WE CAN
USUALLY
UNDERSTAND
THE TRUTH

RICKY CLEMONS

PUBLISHED BY FIDELI PUBLISHING, INC.

ISBN: 978-1-962402-35-4

Published by

Fideli Publishing, Inc.
119 W. Morgan St.
Martinsville, IN 46151

www.FideliPublishing.com

Table of Contents

We Can Usually Understand the Truth

We can usually understand the truth because there is only one way to tell the truth.

Trying to understand a lie can be confusing because a lie can be told in many different ways.

We can usually understand the truth and that can give us a peace of mind.

Trying to understand a lie can trouble our minds.

We can usually understand the truth, which can heal our broken hearts.

Trying to understand a lie can hurt our hearts.

We can usually understand the truth that will set us free from lies.

Trying to understand a lie can put us in the bondage of sin and we can't fully understand how sin will mess us up if we don't confess and repent of our sins unto Jesus Christ, who can save us from our sins.

We can usually understand the truth of God's holy word.

Trying to fully understand sin can surely give us no hope in this sinful world where every lie comes from sin that originated from the devil.

No one can fully understand the sin that Jesus was up against in the wilderness for forty days and forty nights.

That sin fully understood the mission of Jesus to minister to sinners.

Sin fully understood and hated that only Jesus was the living truth to set the captives free from living in sin.

Jesus came to this world to save us from our sins because He fully understood that sin brings death and eternal death upon all sinners.

We all are sinners who don't fully understand that sin can catch us off guard at any time of the day and night and leave us so helpless.

We can usually understand the truth that a child can understand to obey their parents.

A child can feel guilty for lying to their parents, but a child doesn't understand that sin is the root of every lie.

We can usually understand the truth that a fool can understand to not be a lie that comes from sin that we have in our natures every day.

Only Jesus fully understands sin that is in our genes and hereditary tendencies.

We can usually understand the truth that is easy to accept for everyone who loves the truth.

Who in this world can fully understand sin that God hates because He knows that Lucifer misunderstood Him and believed that he was right about God not being worthy to be God?

We can usually understand the truth because there is no misunderstanding about God's love that the devil and his fallen angels and his human agents will try to make to be a lie.

So who can fully understand sin that Jesus fully understood on the cross where He became sin?

That sin fully understood that it failed to conqueror Jesus, who rose from the grave with victory over death.

We can usually understand the truth that is Jesus Christ, who is the way, the truth and the life that is never complicated if we live our lives unto Jesus.

We cannot fully understand sin that will twist and turn us in every wrong direction and will blind our eyes to not see the truth.

We can usually understand the truth when the truth is told to us.

But, who can fully understand sin that every lie comes from?

Jesus fully understood sin and defeated it on the cross to redeem us back to God.

We can't fully understand sin that can come at us in all kinds of ways, but the truth will come at us in only one way and that is Jesus, who is the truth to set us free from the devil's lies.

You and I can't fully understand sin that is the origin of false doctrines and false theories that foolish people believe to be the truth about how we come into existence.

We can usually understand the truth that is at its best in God's holy word, but we can't fully understand sin that Adam and Eve committed against God for believing a lie.

Many people today will misunderstand the truth to be a lie, even with God's holy word that we can't fully understand without the Holy Spirit teaching us all truth.

We can usually understand the truth that can surely cause us to feel so relieved of lies and deceptions that come from sin that brilliant minds can't fully understand for being stained with sin that only the blood of Jesus can wash clean when we confess and repent unto Jesus.

We can usually understand the truth because of Jesus being the light of the world to shine His eternal truth all through our minds and hearts in this dark, sinful world.

If the devil could get rid of all of the truth, he would do that without any hesitation so he could fill this world with nothing but lies.

Lies were Lucifer's biggest sin he committed against God, because he told the angels in heaven that God was unfair to not let him in on the creation of human beings who God created in His likeness.

We can't fully understand sin, even in its smallest form viewed under a microscope.

Sin can spread like the Corona virus that killed millions of people because the corona virus comes from sin and we just didn't understand how it began as we lived in our ignorance of not knowing if we would get the virus.

We can usually understand the truth that can truly give us some comfort because the scientists had comforted our minds when they found an antidote for the corona virus, but we can't fully understand sin that is all about troubling our minds every day.

We can usually understand the truth that was originated by God the Father, the Son and the Holy Spirit, giving understanding to prophets to speak the truth in this dark, sinful world.

We can't fully understand how sin can work its bad effects in us until we reap what we sow from that sin catching up with us.

Sin can surely lead us even to our death if we don't confess and repent of that sin unto Jesus Christ.

We can usually understand the truth that sin has no power over for no one to misunderstand the truth about Jesus Christ who shed His blood and gave up His life on the cross to save us from our sins.

The devil knew that Adam and Eve wouldn't understand the bad effects of their sins that would greatly affect all life and nature in this world that would groan from the absence of God's perfect creation upon this world.

We can usually understand the truth that God told Adam and Eve in the Garden of Eden where they understood the truth but rejected the truth in favor of what they believed to be the truth from the devil who originated sin.

Lucifer didn't even understand sin that he created for rebelling against God who could have vanished Lucifer into thin air, but God didn't do that and gave Lucifer a chance to repent.

Lucifer didn't take the chance God gave him to repent because he didn't understand that he would be lost in his sins forever and ever and burn up in the lake of fire.

Lucifer didn't understand that God means what He says, and Lucifer took God's words for granted and didn't understand all of the truth of God.

We can usually understand the truth when we hear the truth of God's holy word in sermons and Sabbath school lessons in the church that is for every race of people to enter into and worship the Lord Jesus Christ.

No one can fully understand the lies of sin that hates all the truth, especially all the truth of God's holy word that can detect every sin under the microscope of this sinful world.

We can't fully understand sin that can camouflage itself behind billions of faces every day that the truth of God's holy word will sooner or later reveal in everyone's life.

We can usually understand the truth that has no assumptions or opinions about anyone who the truth completely knows every day whether we have mood changes or remain the same way in our life day after day.

We can't ever fully understand sin that has over a thousand ways to distract us from the Lord Jesus Christ if we don't stay in prayer without ceasing to keep our eyes on Jesus day after day.

Only Jesus fully understands sin that He overcame in this world where He humbled Himself unto death to save us from our sins.

The devil doesn't understand the love of God who he rebelled against in heaven.

Lucifer took God's love for him to be weak, so he tried to walk over God which he could not do and was cast out of heaven with one third of the angels following behind him.

You and I can usually understand the truth that will never put us in any kind of bondage, but we will never fully understand sin that makes up all kinds of lies that the truth will set us free from for believing in Jesus Christ.

Jesus is all-powerful to cleanse us from our sins and save us from our sins if we repent and turn to Him.

Jesus understands all things that He created that can't ever rise above Him or His God-given authority over all things seen and unseen.

We can usually understand the truth that is all about Jesus Christ who is the Son of God and the word of God that was made flesh and lived among sinners without sin in His flesh.

We can't fully understand sin that hates people and brings on wars and rumors of wars against God's peaceful nations that sin covets.

We can usually understand the truth that sin can never get rid of with its lies.

Only Jesus fully understands the devil's evil schemes and knows that the devil can change on us so fast on the spur of the moment.

We can't fully understand the wiles of the devil's sins that only Jesus can truly protect us from in many ways that we don't see.

We can usually understand the truth that can be so crystal clear when the Holy Spirit speaks the truth to us, but we can't fully understand sin that will twist up our minds with the devil's lies if we don't spend any time reading the bible to know the truth about Jesus Christ, our only living hope and true lover of our souls to save us from our sins.

We can usually understand the truth that we true Christians love to tell and love to live.

We don't fully understand sin that we can commit against God over and over again.

God's grace is much greater than our sins and gives us undeserved favor with God.

The devil doesn't understand this undeserved favor we get from God who gives us all the opportunity to accept the truth or reject the truth of His holy word.

We can usually understand the truth that God put in even the hearts of children to feel guilty for telling their parents a lie and break the truth of God's Commandments in their hearts.

We don't fully understand sin that has no shame or guilt about murdering our souls, leaving us lost in our sins.

Sin takes great pleasure in trying to confuse and deceive everybody with its lies every day without giving us a break.

We can usually understand the truth that we can't afford to take a break from on any day because sin loves to cause us to misunderstand the truth of God's holy word.

We can usually understand the truth that is all about Jesus Christ who can make us to be a real, true Christian if we love Him with all of our minds, hearts, souls and strength.

We can't fully understand sin that will make us be a phony in many ways if we live in sin that will never be real with us because sin loves to tell us lies every day.

We can usually understand the truth that we can always be sure about to set us free from lying to ourselves so that we can always be true to ourselves.

We can't fully understand sin that is all about lies and death all around the world where God is present to give us good understanding of His truth that is everlasting beyond all sin that God will one day burn up in the lake of fire and brimstone right here on earth.

We can usually understand the truth that shines like the sun in our minds and hearts so that we can discern the truth from a lie.

We can't fully understand that sin is total darkness and can appear to be the light of God's truth that the devil knows so much better than you and me.

Adam and Eve didn't understand sin that disguised itself to be the truth in that unforbidden fruit that Eve and Adam ate in the Garden of Eden.

They were perfect in every way but the devil caused them to misunderstand that with his lie.

We can thank God for His Son, Jesus Christ, who didn't give into sin to save us from our sins because Jesus fully understands the deadly effects of all sin that He became on the cross and was forsaken by God.

Jesus probably felt eternally lost when God had forsaken Him who became the totality of the darkness of all sin that we will never fully understand until we enter into heaven when Jesus comes back again to take us to heaven if we are saved in Him.

We can usually understand the truth that treats everybody right to be set free from lies.

We can't fully understand sin that takes great pleasure in lying on the truth and abusing love to try to cause us to believe that God is not love, especially if God doesn't answer our prayers on our time that can be too soon or too late.

We can't fully understand sin's waywardness that is very destructive over a billion ways, but we can usually understand the truth that loves to heal us from the brokenness of lies that are the crown on the head of sin as it wears the robe of death.

We can usually understand the truth that is our Lord God and Savior Jesus Christ, who we can only worship in spirit and truth.

We can't fully understand sin that fools will worship and not know that sin will laugh really hard and make fun of their fate.

We can usually understand the truth that will stay the same no matter how many times we tell the truth, but we can't fully understand sin that every lie comes from and can change its story more than a thousand times.

We can usually understand the truth that can be so accurate and clear for even a child to understand, but we can't fully understand sin that can surely confuse and deceive the most genius minds to doubt and scorn the truth of God's holy word.

We can usually understand the truth that Jesus Christ is the origin of to set us free from believing lies and living a lie, but we can't fully understand sin that the devil is the origin of to try to bind us up in his bondage of lies.

God gave us a free will for us to choose to believe and live the truth that is all about loving and obeying Jesus Christ, or we can choose to believe and live in sin that is all about the devil and his lies that we can't fully understand.

We can't fully understand how many ways sin can deceive us and kill us who the devil hates.

We can usually understand the truth that only liars will fear because the truth will expose them for who they really are, but we can't fully understand sin that will imitate the truth so many times that we can't count.

We can usually understand the truth that Jesus Christ proclaimed to all the world in God's totality of truth and love that Jesus demonstrated on the cross to save us from our sins.

Nothing in this world can be more truth than the love of God.

The devil and his fallen angels and human agents don't understand this because they are lost in their sins.

We can usually understand the truth that a true Christian will speak and live in love every day.

We can't fully understand sin that takes pleasure in causing us to say and do something wrong, especially on the spur of the moment.

Sin can come at us so swiftly that we can't fully understand, but we can usually understand the truth that is swifter than sin because of Jesus Christ who can answer our prayers faster than our guardian angel can protect us.

We can't fully understand sin that the devil parades in his appearance as an angel of light before us to distract us away from God.

We can usually understand the truth that God gave us a free will to choose to love and obey Jesus Christ or live in sin.

We can't fully understand how deep that sin can take us down into its depths of darkness.

We can usually understand the truth that will sooner or later reveal who we really are being like Jesus or being like the devil.

We can't fully understand sin that came from Lucifer who was the most beautiful and highest angel in heaven.

Lucifer became full of himself and rebelled against God over what was impossible for him to achieve — to be like the most-high God.

We can't fully understand why a perfect angel would flaw his perfection over what was impossible for him to achieve in heaven.

We can usually understand the truth that we will reap what we sow, but we can't fully understand sin that is locked in chains of eternal denial before God.

We can usually understand the truth that we can choose to deny ourselves and pick up our crosses and follow Jesus Christ, who is the way, the truth and the life for us to live every day.

We can't fully understand sin that takes pleasure in causing us to dig our own graves, regardless of whether we're good or bad, because sin will take us down in its darkness of eternal death if we don't repent of our sins and live for Jesus every day.

We can usually understand the truth that can surely keep us on the right course, but we can't fully understand sin that is very shady and will ruin anyone's good reputation even in the church where the wheat and tares grow together for only Jesus to separate.

Jesus fully understands that only He knows how not to pull up a wheat to be a tare, and He can fully understand sin's endless motives that are nothing but nonsense to God.

We can usually understand the truth that is all about Jesus Christ who is merciful to carry us even through the hardships that we can bring on ourselves.

We can't fully understand sin that thrives on making anyone miserable, but we can usually understand the truth that can give us joy to spread the truth of the gospel of Jesus Christ to all the world.

We can usually understand the truth that is always good to speak in love to make this world a much better place to live in.

We can't fully understand that lying evil sin that is all about making this world hard to live in, like what we see and hear on the world news that is rampant with unpleasant words to say and bad things that we see.

We can usually understand the truth that can sharpen and elevate the minds of uneducated people to become bible scholars.

We can't fully understand sin that can cause an educated man and woman to act like fools, as if they don't have a brain in their heads.

We can usually understand the truth that can ease our minds, but we can't fully understand sin that many people will praise and feel no uneasiness in living in their sins that God hates, even as God loves their souls to be saved in His Son, Jesus Christ.

We can usually understand the truth that liars will get very offended by because the truth will reveal their true identities.

We can't fully understand sin that can cause us to not fully understand ourselves who can think, say or do something that we don't understand.

We can usually understand the truth that can be motivating, encouraging and plain for us to hold onto very tight every day.

We can't fully understand sin that takes great pleasure to especially complicate the truth of God's holy word that was written to us in love by holy men who God inspired to write the truth that scoffers very strongly criticize and reject.

We can usually understand the truth that can straighten things out, we can't fully understand sin that can cause us to mess things up.

We can usually understand the truth that enhances and enlightens the mind, but we can't fully understand sin that can ill the body and mind.

We can usually understand the truth that can surely convince the members in our family that you and I are Christians who they have seen down through the years up to this day.

We can't fully understand sin that can wear a mask on its face for years and years and can cause anyone to live proudly and die proudly in an illusion.

We can usually understand the truth that is Jesus Christ our Lord who is the origin of all truth in the heavens and here on earth where the truth is for the good of everyone to worship God in spirit and truth.

We can't fully understand sin that is the origin of adversities, lies, foolishness, demoralizing things and the origin of death that can come upon us so unaware at any time.

We can usually understand the truth that the judge and jury loves to hear in the courtroom, but we can't fully understand sin that can make a lying criminal to be found innocent in the courtroom.

We can usually understand the truth that is Bible prophesy that will be fulfilled, but we can't fully understand sin that mocks all Bible prophecy and loves to degrade humanity.

We can usually understand the truth that will surely be seen in our actions, but we can't fully understand sin that has nothing but bad motives and can be only full of hot air from the tip of the tongue.

We can usually understand the truth that loving people tell in love to have no bad intentions of hurting anyone's feelings with the truth, but we can't fully understand sin that has nothing but bad intentions to hurt anyone's feelings with its lies.

We can usually understand the truth that is the judge of our thoughts, words and actions, but we can't fully understand sin that takes great pride in making a good person look bad and a bad person to look good.

We can usually understand the truth that can surely keep us spiritually awake in this dark, sinful world, but we can't fully understand sin that can cause anyone to spiritually sleep walk in this dark, sinful world where the devil loves to ambush spiritual sleepwalkers who are spiritually unconscious to the truth of God's holy word.

We can usually understand the truth that a prosecutor and a defense lawyer would try to prove their case with the truth in the courtroom where one of them doesn't have the truth but will pretend to have the truth and may still win their case in the courtroom.

We can usually understand the truth that will surely stay the same way every day, but we can't fully understand sin that is prone to change on anyone for for the worse in every evil way.

We can usually understand the truth that is very real with no deceptions and pretense, but we can't fully understand sin that can deceive anyone and can cause a brilliant deceptive person to deceive millions of people.

We can usually understand the truth that will always make very good sense to anyone who loves to hear the truth and live the truth of God's holy word, but we can't fully understand sin that is surely evil and nonsense, especially to God.

We can usually understand the truth that the day will change over into the night and the night will change over into the day in its purity, but we can't fully understand sin that is filled with impurity to cause good weather to change into bad weather and can cause a Christian to change like Dr. Jekyll and Mr. Hyde.

We can usually understand the truth that is all about correcting us when we are wrong and teaching us what is right by God, but we can't fully understand sin that is all about schemes, violence, lust, strife, prejudice, greed, betrayal, unfairness, lawlessness and death because sin breaks God's ten golden rules.

We can usually understand the truth that defines and elevates the courts, but we can't fully understand sin that can downgrade the highest courts of justice that are supposed to fall in line with the truth of God's holy word.

Has a Big Effect on God

What we think has a big effect on God.

What we say has a big effect on God.

What we believe has a big effect on God.

What we eat has a big effect on God.

What we drink has a big effect on God.

How we dress has a big effect on God.

How we treat one another has a big effect on God.

How we treat ourselves has a big effect on God.

How we treat the animals has a big effect on God.

How we treat nature has a big effect on God.

How we treat this world has a big effect on God.

Whatever we do has a big effect on God.

Every choice we make has a big effect on God.

The way we live our lives has a big effect on God every day.

When Lucifer and one third of the angels in heaven rebelled against God, it had a big effect on God who cast them out of heaven.

When Adam and Eve sinned against God, it had a big effect on God who put them out of the Garden of Eden.

When Cain killed his brother Abel, it had a big effect on God who made Cain a fugitive.

When God's Son Jesus Christ was betrayed, it had a big effect on God and meant that Judas would have been better off to never have been born.

When Jesus was spit on, bruised and beaten, it had a big effect on God.

When Jesus was nailed on the cross and died on the cross, it had a big effect on God who felt the pain of the death of His only begotten Son.

The bloodshed of war has a big effect on God, who created us all to love one another and not hurt and kill one another.

Every living soul has a big effect on God, who gave us His Son to save us from our sins.

How we feel has a big effect on God, who will heal our broken hearts.

Every day that we live our lives has an effect on God, who can shorten our lives or prolong our lives according to His reasons that are always right.

There is nothing that doesn't have a big effect on God, who sees all things seen and unseen and knows all things that have a big effect on God who had wonderfully made all things from the beginning of time on earth.

If we believe that whatever we think, say and do doesn't have a big effect on God, then we are only fooling ourselves.

The devil and his fallen angels know too well that our soul salvation has a big effect on God, so the devil tries his best to cause our souls to be lost like he is forever lost.

The devil had no true repentance unto God after he rebelled against God and had a big, negative effect on God who will one day cast him and all of his fallen angels and human agents into the lake of fire.

We can read all through the bible about what people did that had a big effect on God and caused him to bless people or punish people according to the choices they made that God didn't overlook or let slip by Him.

Death has a bigger effect on God than on you and me who God created from the beginning to live forever.

Adam and Eve brought death upon themselves for disobeying God and they brought death upon us all, which has a big effect on God who gave us His Son Jesus Christ to give us eternal life if we believe in Jesus Christ.

Nothing has a big effect on us more than it does God, because everything that exists has a big effect on God, even when we lay down to sleep and don't know what is going on around us.

Every breathing, living creature has a big effect on God, and every living thing has a big effect on God who didn't create any junk from the beginning.

All creatures great and small have their purpose in life that has a big effect on God.

Even the smallest thing has a big effect on God, who doesn't overlook anyone or anything that He can use for His good but the devil will try to use anyone or anything for evil.

Our destiny has a big effect on God, who doesn't choose our destiny for us because He gave us a free will to choose our own destiny, whether we believe in Jesus or believe in the devil.

This whole world has a big effect on God who will one day create a new world of righteous living.

If God is Imaginary

If God is imaginary, then we can burn up all the bibles.

If God is imaginary, then we all can become atheists.

If God is imaginary, then we all wouldn't exist.

If God is imaginary, then we all would be better off never having been born.

If God is imaginary, then every church would be so worthless.

If God is imaginary, then life would be so dead.

If God is imaginary, then hope would be so out of date.

If God is imaginary, then time would be so hopeless.

If God is imaginary, then nothing would be possible.

If God is imaginary, then religion would be so useless.

If God is imaginary, then lies would be so true.

If God is imaginary, then the devil would have the power to kill us all.

If God is imaginary, then we all would be so possessed by the devil.

If God is imaginary, then Jesus Christ would be a fraud.

If God is imaginary, then the truth would be so void.

If God is imaginary, then every human being would be so suicidal.

If God is imaginary, then this whole world would be so inhumane.

If God is imaginary, then the whole universe would be so momentary.

If God is imaginary, then all existence would be so fictional.

If God is imaginary, then all things seen and unseen are only a bluff.

God is forever far from being imaginary because nature itself is also a bible that we can study to know that God is read.

There are many church folks who project God to be imaginary because they live their lives like God is not real.

They live their lives with no renewed life in Jesus Christ, who was a real, sinless man and God in the flesh.

There are many so-called Christians who cause God to be imaginary before unbelievers who see many church folks living in their sins against God.

Many unbelievers see no real change in many so-called Christians making God to be only imaginary because they have no real godly change in their lives and are playing church.

There are many so-called Christians, but they don't stand a chance against a real, true, all-powerful God who is not imaginary to anyone who believes in His Son, Jesus Christ.

Living for Jesus is real and not imaginary in His holy word that is the real, everlasting truth about God the Father, the Son and the Holy Spirit.

If God is imaginary, then every word that comes from the tips of our tongues would be meaningless.

If God is imaginary, then everything that we do would have no substance like the air that we breathe in and out of our nostrils.

If God is imaginary, then heaven is not real, the universe is not real and this world is not real for us to be so imaginary that anyone in their right frame of mind won't claim to be because we love being real in our real bodies that a real God gave to us, even though atheists and evolutionists pretty much doubt this.

Jesus' Bride is His Church

Jesus' bride is His church.

Her love covers a multitude of sins every day that she speaks the love of Jesus and gives that love to everybody.

Her beauty shines like the sun to brighten up everybody's lives in the name of her husband, Jesus Christ.

She goes through the wilderness of life with her eyes stayed on Jesus, who gives her the strength and encouragement that she needs to make it through this life.

Jesus' bride is His church.

Her faith in Jesus withstands the test of time that she cherishes each day in this world to spread the gospel of Jesus Christ.

She falls down at times on the ground of being misunderstood and falsely accused, but her loving husband, Jesus, will waste no time to be there for her and stand her back up with her head up high.

Jesus' bride is His church.

She discerns this world with the word of God that she knows and lives by before the world every day.

She loves Jesus with all of her heart, soul, mind and strength and will never deny her husband, Jesus, before anyone in this world.

She dresses up in holiness and righteousness to draw the right kind of attention which she uses to honor her husband, Jesus, with the utmost respect every day.

Jesus' bride is His Church.

She will joyfully talk about the love of Jesus and how He is always there for her in this sinful and troubled world.

She puts all of her trust in her husband, Jesus, who she knows will give her joy and a peace of mind to live in this world of changing times.

She is very sure and content that Jesus will never take her through any changes for the worse, but will surely do so for the better so she can be more and more like Jesus.

Jesus' bride is His church.

Her prayers unto Jesus are true and sincere with humility of confession and repentance and healing that she knows she needs to empty herself to be filled with the Holy Spirit.

She makes her calling to be very sure that she works out her soul's salvation by examining herself to be like Jesus every day.

She has no doubt that her husband, Jesus, is holy, righteous and perfect in every word that He says and everything that He does for her to win souls to Him who is always so faithful and true to her that she has no reason to ever doubt.

Jesus' bride is His church.

She sometimes stumbles and gets weary for living in this sinful world that she takes no pleasure in because she believes that Jesus is coming back again to take her to heaven to live with Him forever and ever.

She knows that Jesus will put stars on her crown for winning souls to Him, even souls who she never sees in this world.

She knows that she can always fall back on Jesus who is there to catch her when she is blinded by many of her own spiritual brothers and sisters who proclaim to be a Christian and don't bear fruit of the Holy Spirit.

Jesus' bride is His church.

She loves to stay spiritually awake in this sinful world that loves to try to cause her to fall spiritually asleep when her husband, Jesus, is coming back to this world like a thief in the night.

She knows that she is all secured in Jesus' almighty hands that will hold her together no matter what trials and persecutions come her way.

She knows that her strong foundation is Jesus, who she can always stand on because Jesus will never lose His strong foundation in any storm that will come her way.

She knows without a doubt that she is happily married to the Son of God who gave this world His only begotten Son to redeem everyone back to God.

Jesus' bride is His church.

She invites everyone into her house and feeds them with the bread of life, who is her husband, Jesus, who supplies all of her needs to win souls to Him.

She knows what it means to love Jesus and keep His Commandments that won't burden her down but will set her free from spiritual adultery.

Jesus' bride is His glorious church that He adorns in His heavenly Father's everlasting love.

She gladly makes her choice to deny herself and pick up her cross to follow Jesus all the way through the thick and thin of her life and through the good days and bad days of her life that she knows is in Jesus' almighty hands.

She can never say and believe that Jesus let her slip out of His hands that keep a tight grip on her every day, no matter when she can't see where she is going like a blind person.

When she gets weary, Jesus strengthens her to stay on the strait and narrow road to keep her from getting on the road of destruction.

She loves everybody like Jesus loves everybody.

She is the greatest wife and the greatest mother and the greatest friend to spiritually nurture souls to believe in her husband, Jesus, who will save any soul who confesses and repents and turns to Him before it's too late.

Jesus' bride is His faithful and loving church that is not in vain because of Jesus, who took away the devil's power over this world when he died on the cross for our sins and rose from the grave with victory over death and the grave.

Jesus has made His bride to be victorious in Him who said in His holy word that the world will hate His church because the world hated Him for speaking the truth of God and living the truth of God.

Jesus' bride is His remnant church.

She knows not to judge anyone before Jesus comes back again because she knows that her mission in this life is to love souls and win souls to Jesus.

When Jesus takes her to heaven for a thousand years, Jesus will allow her to judge the fallen angels and every lost soul for her to truly know that God is an everlasting and fair God to all of His creations.

She knows what it means to pray without ceasing and to be watchful for Jesus coming back again like the five wise virgins who kept their lamps burning to meet their bridegrooms.

With His Everlasting Love

God loves you and me with His everlasting love no matter how much we mess up in life.

No matter how bad off we are, God loves you and me with His everlasting love.

God doesn't hold grudges against you and me for doing Him wrong, which we all do in one way or another way.

God loves you and me with His everlasting love that God gives to us through His Son, Jesus Christ.

Even if you and I tell lie after lie and pretend to be who we are not, God loves you and me with His everlasting love.

God's everlasting love hovers over you and me every day like the great blue sky showing you and me how special we are to Him.

It hurts God's heart when we are hurting from life's disappointments and griefs that are no comparison to God's everlasting love for you and me.

God doesn't want you and me to be lost in our sins — that breaks God's heart.

You and I can't ever imagine how much God loves us with His everlasting love that you and I can hold onto real tight every day.

God loves you and me with His everlasting love that will get us through any hardships in this life.

We must trust God, who is every good thing to us because God will never let us down.

If we repent and turn to God's Son, Jesus Christ, Jesus will fill our lives with unspeakable love.

Only You, My Lord

Only You, my Lord, can make something bad in my life to be for my good.

When something bad happens to me, only You, my Lord, can make it be for my good.

I surely can't make something bad in my life be for my good because only You, my Lord Jesus Christ, have the power to do that.

I will fail to make that accomplishment to make a bad thing in my life to be a good thing for me.

Who am I to keep something bad from happening to me on any day when Jesus has complete power and control over the good and bad things in this world?

I know that I am so blessed by the Lord, who won't put on me more than what I can bear.

If the Lord allows something bad to happen to me, He knows that I can bear it and will give Him all the glory and praise for bringing me through a bad thing in my life.

When something bad happens to me, it will get the best of me if I don't pray to Jesus and ask Him to give me the strength to bear it.

Only Jesus can make something bad in my life to be for my good, so I trust Him to bring me through that bad thing.

The Lord is so merciful to me to allow me to recover from bad things that try to weaken my faith in the Lord.

The Lord gave me the free will choice to choose to live for Him no matter what bad things come my way.

I can choose not to fall apart in despair when something bad happens to me because I know that I can pray to Jesus and put my Hope in Him no matter what bad thing happens to me.

I am still alive today because of God's mercy and grace that have brought me through all the bad things in my life.

Only You, my Lord Jesus, can make something bad in my life to be for my good so that I can be a witness of You before my neighbors.

To Be About

Many people will make this world to be about white people.

Many people will make this world to be about Asian people.

Many people will make this world to be about Spanish people.

Many people will make this world to be about Russian people.

Many people will make this world to be about German people.

Many people will make this world to be about Black people.

Many people will make this world to be about Indian people.

Many people will make this world to be about Jewish people.

Many people will make this world to be about Arab people.

Many people will make this world to be about American people.

Many people will make this world to be about European people.

Many people will make this world to be about Brazilian people.

Many people will make this world to be about African people.

Many people will make this world to be about Australian people.

Many people will make this world to be about Eskimo people.

Many people will make this world to be about Pakistani people.

Many people will make this world to be about Japanese people.

Many people will make this world to be about Chinese people.

Jesus will make heaven to be about every race of people going with Him to heaven when he comes back again.

Jesus will raise the righteous dead who will be people of every race who were saved in Him.

Jesus will make heaven to be about every skin color of people entering into heaven for being saved in Him, whether we're alive when Jesus comes back or we're raised from the dead to be taken up on the clouds of glory.

Giving Jesus Your Best

As long as you know you are giving Jesus your best, you don't need to worry about how other people feel and what they say about you.

There will always be some church folks who won't believe you are giving Jesus your best.

No one knows you like you and Jesus day after day, and Jesus knows your weaknesses and strengths.

Only Jesus always knows what is your best, certainly much better than anyone else can know.

You pretty much know what you can do and can't do day after day.

You might give your spouse, children and friends your best and they may not appreciate it.

You might give your best to your boss on your job and he or she may not appreciate it.

If you give Jesus your best, Jesus and all the angels in heaven will appreciate it.

Jesus will truly bless you for giving Him your best.

You might give your church family your best, but there may be some church folks who will criticize and degrade your best efforts.

They don't know you like Jesus knows you completely, because only Jesus is worthy to judge your best.

Giving Jesus your best will surely please Him and will keep you going strong in Him.

You can give people your best but there are always some people who will be displeased by your best.

There are people who know that you are giving them your best and they will take advantage of you and cause you to overwork yourself.

Jesus will never overwork you for giving Him your best.

Jesus will truly bless you for doing your best, but there are people who will use your best against you.

Your motives and intentions can be good for giving people your best, but there are people who will take you doing your best as a threat to them.

You can always give Jesus your best and He will never take it in the wrong way like people can do and give you a bad name.

Giving Jesus your best from your heart is a great thing that no one can take away from you no matter how much they take your best in the wrong way.

As long as Jesus is pleased with your best, that is all that really matters because Jesus has a heaven to take you to when He comes back again.

No One is Alone in this World

No one is alone in this world because the choices that we make will affect one another in some kind of way.

No one is alone in this world because everyone will be in the presence of someone sooner or later, no matter being good or bad.

No one is alone in this world where everyone has a mother and father who procreated and caused them to live in this world where everyone needs some kind of help from someone no matter being good or bad.

The Lord didn't create human beings to be alone because God is the origin of relationships and community that everyone in this world needs every day.

Anyone in their right mind won't be happy about wanting to be all alone because that truly won't prosper anyone to be in a relationship with the Lord.

God is never alone up in heaven where the holy angels surround Him as He sits on His holy throne.

God doesn't leave us alone to ourselves, even though we are prone to make a bad choice whether we know it or not.

God always reaches out to us first to let us know that we are not alone in this world to wander through life with no purpose, because our purpose is to love God and keep His Commandments.

No one is alone in this world and left to themselves because God's love is for everyone to receive and share with one another, which we can only do through Jesus Christ.

No one can ever be so alone like Jesus was on the cross to say to His heavenly Father, "God, why has thou forsaken me?"

Jesus experienced the worst kind of being alone to save us from our sins that Jesus became on the cross and could not bear His heavenly Father turning His back on Him.

No one is alone in this world to say or believe that God doesn't love them, because God gave us His only begotten Son to redeem us back to Him who has an eternal community in heaven.

No one is so alone in this world that God doesn't see and reach out to have a relationship with you.

God is always joyful to be in a relationship with us if we just choose to trust Him to fill our lives with love for one another so we don't feel alone.

No one is alone in the world because God gives His grace to everyone to be saved in His Son, Jesus Christ.

Everyone in their right mind can choose Jesus over the false belief of being alone and all by themselves.

Everyone is loved by God and will answer to God, who leaves no one alone by themselves for as long as we live.

I Want to be Caught Up in You, My Lord

I want to be caught up in You, my Lord Jesus Christ, who gives me the strength to keep going on day after day.

O Lord, I thank You for Your blessings upon my life, but I don't want to be caught up in Your blessings upon my life.

I want to be caught up in You, my Lord Jesus Christ, who answers my prayers that I don't deserve for not always waiting on You who is always on time to be there for me.

I don't want to be caught up in Your blessings, my Lord, because your blessings can't forgive me of my sins.

My Lord, Your blessings can't save me from my sins.

My Lord, Your blessings can't cleanse me of my sins.

I want to be caught up in You, my Lord and Savior Jesus Christ, who can forgive me of my sins, save me from my sins and cleanse me of my sins if I confess and repent and turn to You, my Lord Jesus Christ, which I can only do one day at a time.

I want to be caught up in You, my Lord Jesus Christ, who I need to keep my eyes on every day.

I don't want to keep my eyes on Your blessings, my Lord Jesus Christ, because Your blessings can blind my spiritual eyes to not see that I need to always keep my relationship with you, my Lord.

I don't want to be caught up in Your blessings, my Lord, because Your blessings can't relate to me like You, my Lord, who can always relate to me no matter what I go through in my life.

I want to always be caught up in You, my Lord Jesus Christ, because only You can give me Your Holy Spirit to convict me of my sins and convert my life for me to live it unto You.

I don't want to be caught up in Your blessings, my Lord, because Your blessings can't give me Your Holy Spirit.

It's so easy for anyone to get caught up in Your blessings, my Lord, while not giving You the glory and praise.

All good things come from You, my Lord, and all blessings are from You.

Every true saint will not put their blessings above You, my Lord.

Every true saint knows what it means to be caught up in You, my Lord Jesus Christ, because Your blessings are only a shadow moving where You tell it to go.

I want to be caught up in You, my Lord Jesus Christ, because You can give me a peace of mind, while being caught up in Your blessings will surely be dissatisfying to me and make me not be content with the blessings you give to me, my Lord and Savior Jesus Christ.

Can Seem Like Forever

Pain can seem like forever while we feel the pain.

Trouble can seem like forever while we are in trouble.

Heartache can seem like forever while we have the heartache.

Poverty can seem like forever while we are in the poverty.

Fear can seem like forever while we are in the fear.

Grief can seem like forever while we are in the grief.

Discouragement can seem like forever while we are in the discouragement.

Sickness can seem like forever while we are sick.

Good health can seem like forever while we are in good health.

Life can seem like forever while we live.

Time can seem like forever while we have the time.

Misfortune can seem like forever while we have misfortune.

Peace can seem like forever while we have peace.

War can seem like forever while we are in the war.

Love can seem like forever while we are in love.

This world can seem like forever while we live in this sinful world.

Injustice can seem like forever while we are not being treated right.

Prejudice can seem like forever while people discriminate against us.

Stress can seem like forever while we feel the stress.

It's for sure that Jesus Christ lives forever above and beyond this temporary world where nothing lasts forever.

We will one day live forever and ever with Jesus if we are saved in Him who will come back again on the clouds of glory one day to take us to heaven where forever never ends in Jesus Christ.

The hardships that we go through can seem like forever while we are in our hardships, but joy cometh in Jesus Christ if we have trust in Him to get us through our hardships.

Joy is eternal in God's everlasting love.

Nothing in our lives is too big for God to not remove from our lives.

You and I can choose to come to God with all of our hearts, no matter how broken in sin we are.

No matter how deep in sin we are, God won't turn away His everlasting love from you and me who are not too lost for God's Son to save us from our sins if we repent and live for God's Son, Jesus Christ.

The Things in this World

The things in this world can rust and erode.

The things in this world can wear out and fade.

The things in this world can wear down and deteriorate.

The things in this world won't always last.

The things in this world can need repair work.

The things in this world are temporary.

The things in this world are so untrustworthy.

The things in this world can stress us out.

The things in this world can give us a headache.

The things in this world can make us ill.

The things in this world are nothing we can always hold onto.

The things in this world can get us down.

The things in this world can make us unhappy.

The things in this world can let us down.

We must lay up our treasures in heaven where everything is eternal to last forever and ever.

The things in heaven will never rust and erode.

The things in heaven will never wear out and fade.

The things in heaven will never wear down and deteriorate.

The things in heaven will last forever.

The things in heaven will never need any repair work.

The things in heaven are eternally trustworthy.

The things in this world will never fulfill us, but the things in heaven will fulfill our lives forever and ever through our Lord and Savior Jesus Christ, who was heaven on earth in the flesh without sin.

It's Not Me, It's the Lord

It's not me, it's the Lord who brought me this far in my life.

I know that I didn't bring myself this far in my life.

It's not me, it's the Lord who is keeping me alive.

I know that I am not keeping myself alive.

It's not me, it's the Lord who supplies all of my needs.

I know that I don't supply all of my needs.

It's not me, it's the Lord who gives me good thoughts.

I know that I don't give myself good thoughts.

It's not me, it's the Lord who gives me good words to say.

I know that I don't give myself good words to say.

It's not me, it's the Lord who gives me good deeds.

I know that I don't give myself good deeds.

It's not me, it's the Lord who gives me air to breathe.

I know that I don't give myself air to breathe.

It's not me, it's the Lord who gives me strength in my body.

I know that I don't give myself strength in my body.

It's not me, it's the Lord who protects me from unknown harm and danger.

I know that I don't protect myself from unknown harm and danger.

It's not me, it's the Lord who gives me the victory.

I know that I don't give myself the victory.

It's not me, it's the Lord who gives me wisdom.

I know that I don't' give myself wisdom.

It's not me, it's the Lord who gives me common sense.

I know that I don't' give myself common sense.

It's not me, it's the Lord who gives me discernment.

I know that I don't give myself discernment.

It's not me, it's the Lord who gives me peace of mind.

I know that I don't give myself peace of mind.

It's not me, it's the Lord who owns me.

I know that I don't own myself.

It's not me, it's the Lord who gave me knowledge.

I know I didn't give myself knowledge.

It's not me, it's the Lord who gave me a mind

I didn't give myself a mind.

It's not me, it's the Lord who gave me a heart.

I know I didn't give myself a heart.

It's not me, it's the Lord who gave me the free will to choose.

I know I didn't give myself the free will to choose.

It's not me, it's the Lord who gave me His Holy Spirit.

I know I didn't give myself the Holy Spirit.

It's not me, it's the Lord who gave me salvation.

I know I didn't give myself salvation.

It's not me, it's the Lord who has given me the truth.

I know that I didn't give myself the truth.

It's not me, it's the Lord who has given me grace.

I know that I didn't give myself grace.

It's not me, it's the Lord who has given me unspeakable joy.

I know that I didn't give myself unspeakable joy.

It's not me, it's the Lord Jesus Christ who has given me God's love.

I know that I didn't give myself God's love.

It's not me, it's the Lord who winked his eye at my ignorance.

I know that I didn't wink my eye at my ignorance.

It's not me, it's the Lord who never failed me.

I know that I have failed myself.

It's not me, it's the Lord who will always love me.

I know that I didn't always love myself.

It's not me, it's the Lord who can work everything out for my good.

I know that I can't work everything out for my good.

It's not me, it's the Lord who opened my eyes to see the devil's lies.

I know that I didn't open my eyes to see the devil's lies.

It's not me, it's the Lord who is keeping me going strong in Him.

I know that I can't keep myself going strong in the Lord.

It's not me, it's the Lord who has a heaven to put me in.

I know that I don't have a heaven to put myself in.

It's not me, it's the Lord Jesus Christ who will give me eternal life for being saved in Him.

I know that I can't save myself through good works that I do because they can't give me eternal life.

It's not me, it's the Lord who can cleanse me of my sins.

I know that I can't cleanse myself of my sins.

It's not me, it's the Lord who can forgive me of my sins.

I know that I can't forgive myself of my sins.

It's not me, it's the Lord who can save me from my sins.

I know that I can't save myself from my sins.

It's not me, it's the Lord who is worthy to be praised.

I know that I am not worthy to be praised.

It's not me, it's the Lord who has no sins.

I know that I have sins to confess and repent unto the Lord.

It's not me, it's the Lord who cannot lie.

I know that I can tell a lie and live a lie.

It's not me, it's the Lord who knows all things.

I know that I don't know anything compared to everything that the Lord knows.

It's not me, it's the Lord who sees all things.

I know that I am blind compared to the all-seeing Lord.

It's not me, it's the Lord who never fails.

I know that I can fail to do even some simple little things.

It's not me, it's the Lord who lives forever and ever.

I know that I will one day die, and that could be any day before the Lord Jesus Christ comes back again on the clouds of glory.

It's not me, it's the Lord who will raise me from the dead if I am saved in Him.

I know that when I die I can't raise myself from the dead and I can't take myself to heaven because that's something only the Lord can do.

If We Are Not Ready

The Lord truly knows if we are not ready for more people to join the church.

Why would the Lord allow the church to grow if the people in the church are not coming together on one accord?

If a brother or sister in the church receives an honor, then everybody in the church should be happy for their brother or sister in the Lord.

If a brother or sister in the church is suffering, then everybody in the church should suffer with their brother or sister in the Lord.

If we don't come together on one accord in the church body of Jesus Christ, then why would we want more people to join our church?

People would see that we are not being like Jesus if they join our church and we are not on one accord.

In the church, you and I must be like Jesus to one another and not take one another for granted.

We are obligated to be in church.

We all have a free will choice to come to church and worship the Lord Jesus Christ, not to worship anyone in the church.

The Lord Jesus Christ truly knows if we are prepared to receive new members in the church because He is the head of the church, not the pastor, elders or deacons.

We want new members in the church, but we must love everybody who is already in the church where Jesus is not about organizing a circle of friends with certain people in the church.

We who are already in the church can easily believe that we are ready to see the growth with more people.

If the Lord was to bring a lot more people into the church while we are not prepared for it and aren't being like Jesus towards one another, then those people may very well push us out of the church.

What heavy blow that would be for us to be shaken out of the church for not being like Jesus, who tells us that we must love one another to be his disciples.

If we are only happy for certain people in the church, then we are not like Jesus and are not ready for the church to grow in membership.

If we only want to suffer with certain people in their grief, then we are not like Jesus, who will not put up with a divided church body that is not like Him.

Jesus is happy for everyone who receives honor in the church to glorify His holy name.

Jesus suffers with everyone who grieves in the church because Jesus is head of the church and will separate the wheat from the tares.

The Lord truly knows if we are not ready to build up the church.

We cannot do that if we don't have love for one another that people will see when they come into the church.

How can we be ready for the church to grow in membership if we are talking bad about one another and not treating one another right?

If any church grows in membership, it's because of Jesus Christ who knows all of His true children in every church to be a blessing to newcomers in the church.

We All

We all are prone to make some mistakes in our lives.

We all will not always get it right.

We all will feel some stress.

We all won't say the right words all the time.

We all won't think right all the time.

We all won't have the right motives all the time.

We all won't have the right intentions all the time.

We all will make choices.

We all have a brain.

We all have a heart.

We all need to eat food to live.

We all need to drink water to live.

We all need to wear clothes.

We all need to have good hygiene.

We all were once in our mother's womb.

We all were born in sin to have a sinful nature that will cause us all to sin against God.

We all are sinners saved through God's grace.

We all need Jesus Christ.

We all need to love and obey Jesus Christ.

We all must deny ourselves and pick up our crosses to follow Jesus Christ.

We all need to go to a church that Jesus is the head of.

We all need to study and live by God's holy word.

We all are in the presence of an omniscient God.

We all need the Holy Spirit.

We all belong to God.

We are all nothing without Jesus Christ.

We all are hopeless without Jesus Christ.

We all are slaves to sin without Jesus Christ who will cleanse us all from our sins if we confess and repent of our sins and turn to God.

We all have a guardian angel who the Lord God appointed to us all.

We all will reap what we sow.

We all will die one day if Jesus Christ doesn't come back again during our lifetime in the land of the living.

We all need some help sometimes.

We all need some encouragement.

We all are not ignorant of God's ten Commandments and if we don't keep them, God will hold us all accountable.

We all will be judged by God, whether we are good or bad, sane or insane, healthy or sick, knowledgeable or ignorant, rich or poor, young, middle-aged or old.

One day we all will face God in heaven or hell and nowhere in-between.

As Though We

We can eat food as though we can't gain weight.

We can talk as though we are alone for no one to hear us.

We can hear as though we are deaf to what someone says to us.

We can see as though someone is invisible to us.

We can wear clothes as though we have no clothes to wear.

We can sleep as though we are conscious to see our dreams and grab onto them.

We can smile as though no one will notice it.

We can do something as though we didn't move at all.

We can be silent as though we spoke many words.

We can find something as though we never lost it.

We can lose something as though we never had it.

We can clap our hands as though we have no joy.

We can spend money as though we never had it.

We can have knowledge as though we are ignorant.

We can have common sense as though it is no good use to us.

We can go to church as though it doesn't exist.

We can know the truth of God's holy word as though it has no good effect on us.

We can misrepresent Jesus Christ as though Jesus won't hold us accountable.

We can live our lives and one day die as though we were never born to live.

We can live our lives as though we own them and not Jesus, who also owns the afterlife in heaven.

Jesus will take all of His righteous children to heaven when He comes back again on the clouds of glory as though we never lived in this sinful world.

The Best of Christians

The best of Christians have problems.

The best of Christians have struggles.

The best of Christians have issues.

The best of Christians have bad habits.

The best of Christians make mistakes.

The best of Christians have flaws.

The best of Christians fall short of the glory of God.

The best of Christians have sins to confess and repent of.

The best of Christians can turn their backs on Jesus Christ.

The best of Christians can fall down into sin.

The best of Christians can backslide.

The best of Christians can straddle the fence.

The best of Christians can compromise on their faith.

The best of Christians can do something wrong.

The best of Christians can say something wrong.

The best of Christians can have the wrong motives.

The best of Christians can have the wrong intentions.

The best of Christians can be deceived.

The best of Christians can doubt the Lord.

The best of Christians can take their eyes off the Lord.

Elijah was one of the best Christians who ran away from Jezebel because he had doubt that the Lord could protect him from her fury.

Peter was one of the best Christians who denied Jesus three times because he was afraid to say that he was one of Jesus' disciples to keep from being killed.

The best of Christians will mean you and me good and well, but only Jesus is perfect in all of His ways, which is why you and I need to keep our eyes stayed on Jesus.

We can't keep our eyes stayed on the best of Christians who need to be prayed for every day just like you and me because the devil will especially attack the best of Christians with his worst temptations.

Jesus made a way for the best of Christians to escape the devil's worst temptations with the word of God.

Even the weakest Christians can be victorious in Jesus because of being cleansed in the blood of Jesus Christ.

The weakest Christian can truly pray with faith as big as a mustard seed for Jesus to remove the mountains of their doubts and fears and discouragements.

What is Best for Us

The Lord knows what is best for us, even though it can hurt us sometimes when the Lord doesn't give us what we ask Him for.

The Lord knows what is best for us, because the Lord will not give us false hopes like people can do to be our discouragement on any day.

The Lord knows what is best for us, who can ask the Lord for things that the Lord knows we don't need.

The Lord knows what is best for us, because the Lord will always see what we don't see down the road that the Lord knows to be a dead-end when we don't know that.

The Lord knows what is best for us, who don't always know what we are asking the Lord to give us.

The Lord knows if we are ready and strong enough to receive what we ask Him for.

You and I may not have the slightest clue what we ask the Lord to give us, but the Lord always knows what is best for us.

There are times when we put our foot in our mouth and ask the Lord to give us things that the Lord knows wouldn't be good for us.

The Lord always knows what is best for you and me, who don't know what the Lord always knows to protect us from harming and ruining ourselves.

The Lord always knows what is best for us and won't always give us what we ask Him for.

The Lord knows that we don't always pay attention to His warnings about the hidden dangers of not always realizing what we pray and ask Him for.

The Lord always knows what is best for us, even though we can feel like the Lord is wrong for not giving us what we ask Him for.

We are truly wrong for insulting the Lord by feeling like He is wrong when the Lord always knows what is best for us.

If the Lord Jesus Christ gave us everything we pray and ask Him for, then we might very well believe that He is our puppet on a string that we can maneuver any kind of way we want.

The Lord always knows what is best for us, who can easily believe that we are always asking the Lord for the right things.

We can be so wrong for doubting the Lord about anything that He refuses to give to us who don't always know what is best for us.

The Debate Over Our Souls

The devil loves to debate with God, but the devil lost his debate with God up in heaven when God cast him out.

The devil debated with God over the death and resurrection of Jesus Christ.

The devil hated that Jesus died on the cross and rose from the grave to save us from our sins to fulfill God's love for us.

The devil is still debating today about God not existing so atheists can be right in saying there is no God.

The devil debated with God to tell Jesus to come down off the cross because the devil knew he was a defeated foe for seeing Jesus taking on all of our sins for us to be made right with God through the righteousness of Jesus Christ.

God has won the debate with the devil, who will have to burn in hell's fire and brimstone for our sins if we are saved in Jesus Christ.

God has won the debate over our souls, but God has given us all the free will choice to choose to repent and believe in His Son, Jesus Christ.

The debate over our souls is the greatest debate that no one in this world can ever top because only God the Father, the Son and the Holy Spirit can win the debate with the devil over our souls.

Even though the devil lost his debate thousands of years ago, he is still refusing to believe it, and today he is attacking with his temptations at full force.

God has won the debate over our souls, but it is up to you and me to claim our souls in Jesus' name.

We must make Jesus our choice that the devil has no power over because God had predestined to win the debate over our souls to be saved in His Son, Jesus Christ, if we repent and believe in Jesus Christ.

When We Really Get Down to the Truth

When we really get down to the truth, a lot of people don't want to hear the truth.

When we really get down to the truth, a lot of people won't accept the truth.

When we really get down to the truth, a lot of people hate the truth.

When we really get down to the truth, it can hurt our hearts.

When we really get down to the truth, a lot of people are threatened by the truth.

When we really get down to the truth, a lot of people are afraid of the truth.

When we really get down to the truth, a lot of people will cover up the truth.

When we really get down to the truth, a lot of people will criticize the truth.

When we really get down to the truth, a lot of people won't own up to the truth.

When we really get down to the truth, a lot of people will degrade the truth.

When we really get down to the truth, a lot of people will corrupt the truth.

When we really get down to the truth, a lot of people will get rid of the truth.

When we really get down to the truth, a lot of people will downsize the truth.

When we really get down to the truth, a lot of people will mock the truth.

When we really get down to the truth, a lot of people will lie on the truth.

When we really get down to the truth, a lot of people will lie to the truth.

When we really get down to the truth, a lot of people will underestimate the truth.

When we really get down to the truth, a lot of people will make excuses to the truth.

When we really get down to the truth, a lot of people will misunderstand the truth.

When we really get down to the truth, a lot of people will disqualify the truth.

When we really get down to the truth, a lot of people will scorn the truth.

When we really get down to the truth, a lot of people will disrespect the truth.

When we really get down to the truth, a lot of people will terrorize the truth.

When we really get down to the truth, a lot of people will interrupt the truth.

When we really get down to the truth, a lot of people will put down the truth.

When we really get down to the truth, a lot of people will not face up to the truth.

When we really get down to the truth, a lot of people will opinionate the truth.

When we really get down to the truth, a lot of people will be prejudiced against the truth.

When we really get down to the truth, a lot of people will enslave the truth.

When we really get down to the truth, a lot of people will despise the truth.

When we really get down to the truth, a lot of people will pollute the truth.

When we really get down to the truth, a lot of people will delusion the truth.

When we really get down to the truth of God's holy word, the truth will set us free.

When we really get down to the truth of God's holy word, the Holy Spirit will teach us all the truth about Jesus Christ, who is the everlasting truth.

When we really get down to the truth of God's holy word, all the truth in this world is secured in God's holy word that will never change because of Jesus Christ, who is the word of God.

When we really get down to the truth of God's holy word, a lot of people will add their lies to the truth of God's holy word.

When we really get down to the truth of God's holy word, only a few Christian people out of billions of people will live the truth of God's holy word for believing in Jesus Christ, who is the way, the truth and the life to live.

Only if You Allow Things to Go Right

Things will go right, O Lord, only if You allow things to go right.

I can't make anything go right, O Lord, because I have no power on my own to make things go right in my life from day to day.

A bad day can come my way on any day and I have no control over what a day will bring me, O Lord.

Things will go right, O Lord, only if you allow things to go right.

Anything can go wrong at any time of the day and night, and I have no control over that.

Only You, O Lord, can truly bring me through trouble that can come my way on any day.

I have no control over what a day will bring me, O Lord.

Things will go right, O Lord, only if You allow things to go right.

Anything can go wrong at any time of the day and night and I have no control over that.

Only You, O Lord, can truly bring me though trouble that can come my way so unpredictable.

Life can turn me upside-down and life can beat me up, but You, O Lord, truly know how to stand me right-side up and heal my beat-up wounds on Your perfect time.

Things will go right, O Lord, only if You allow things to go right no matter how hard the devil knocks me down.

O Lord, You will pick me up and carry me to Your safe haven while you work the bad things out in my life.

The devil is all about making things go wrong, especially in every Christian's life that You, O Lord, keep in Your heavenly treasure chest.

Things will go right, O Lord, only if you allow things to go right, which You do to outweigh the wrongs that You won't allow to always last.

If We Look At

If we look at our problems and don't look at what the Lord can do for us, then our problems will get the best of us.

If we look at people and not what the Lord can do for us, then people will get the best of us.

If we look at our finances and not what the Lord can do for us, then our finances will get the best of us.

If we look at our mistakes and not what the Lord can do for us, then our mistakes will get the best of us.

If we look at our bad habits and not what the Lord can do for us, then our bad habits will get the best of us.

If we look at our bad situations and not what the Lord can do for us, then our bad situations will get the best of us.

If we look at our failures and not what the Lord can do for us, then our failures will get the best of us.

If we look at our discouragements and not what the Lord can do for us, then our discouragements will get the best of us.

If we look at our grief and not what the Lord can do for us, then our grief will get the best of us.

If we look at our doubts and not what the Lord can do for us, then our doubts will get the best of us.

If we look at our enemies and not what the Lord can do for us, then our enemies will get the best of us.

If we look at ourselves and not what the Lord can do for us, then ourselves will get the best of us.

We need to always look at what the Lord can do for us who can't do ourselves or anyone else any good if we don't keep our eyes on the Lord, whose goodness leads us to repent of our sins and turn to Him.

No Matter Where You Go

No matter where you go, your thoughts will go with you.

No matter where you go, your words will go with you.

No matter where you go, your good deeds will go with you.

No matter where you go, your bad deeds will go with you.

No matter where you go, your joy will go with you.

No matter where you go, your sadness will go with you.

No matter where you go, your love will go with you.

No matter where you go, your hatred will go with you.

No matter where you go, your peace will go with you.

No matter where you go, your strife will go with you.

No matter where you go, your brilliance will go with you.

No matter where you go, your intelligence will go with you.

No matter where you go, your common sense will go with you.

No matter where you go, your talents will go with you.

No matter where you go, your skills will go with you.

No matter where you go, your mind will go with you.

No matter where you go, your heart will go with you.

No matter where you go, your feelings will go with you.

No matter where you go, your kindness will go with you.

No matter where you go, your respect will go with you.

No matter where you go, your truth will go with you.

No matter where you go, your lies will go with you.

No matter where you go, your lifestyle will go with you.

No matter where you go, your sins will go with you.

No matter where you go, your greed will go with you.

No matter where you go, your corruption will go with you.

No matter where you go, your realness will go with you.

No matter where you go, your pretense will go with you.

No matter where you go, your rebellion will go with you.

No matter where you go, your habits will go with you.

No matter where you go, your health will go with you.

No matter where you go, your lust will go with you.

No matter where you go, your pride will go with you.

No matter where you go, your self-esteem will go with you.

No matter where you go, your jealousy will go with you.

No matter where you go, your prejudice will go with you.

No matter where you go, your evil will go with you.

No matter where you go, your education will go with you.

No matter where you go, your knowledge will go with you.

No matter where you go, your ignorance will go with you.

No matter where you go, your religion will go with you.

No matter where you go, your faith in Jesus Christ will go with you.

No matter where you go, your spiritual gifts will go with you.

No matter where you go, your obedience unto Jesus will go with you.

No matter where you go, your love for Jesus will go with you.

Every Generation is Different

Every generation is different and will not see eye to eye on everything.

Every generation of people will do some things in a different way.

The generation before our generation didn't have the technology that our generation has today.

The next generation will have even better technology than our generation today.

Every generation of people will not have the same fashions; those change in every generation.

Every generation of people will not have the same lifestyles; those change in every generation.

Every generation of people will not have the same ideas; those change in every generation.

Even in the church, every generation of Christians will come up with some new ideas to win souls to our Lord and Savior Jesus Christ.

Even though every generation is different in some ways, God will not change His holy word — that will stay the same in every generation of people.

Generations will change, but the Lord God is the same yesterday, today and tomorrow.

The past generations, the present generation and the future generations can't change God's mind and make Him change His holy ten Commandments.

God's Commandments are for every generation of people to keep and we will keep them if we love Jesus Christ.

Through All of My Hardships

O Lord, I thank You for bringing me through all of the hardships in my life to mold me and shape me into the being you have blessed me to be in loving You and keeping Your Commandments.

O Lord, You brought me safely through my hardships that You didn't allow to kill me, even though I had brought some hardships upon myself by living in my sins against You.

O Lord, I thank You for bringing me through all of my past hardships to make me strong in doing Your holy will today.

My hardships were only like a dream passing through my deep sleep in the night when You, O Lord, woke me up spiritually to see Your shining light of truth setting me free from the darkness of the devil's lies and deceit.

O Lord, I thank You for bringing me safely through all the hardships in my life so that I can truly know today that You didn't give up on me who gave up on myself.

You brought me this far in my life for me to not be ignorant about Your miraculous love for me.

O Lord, I thank You for bringing me through all of my hardships that were only for a moment in my life that belongs to You who no hardships can defeat.

We Can Say, "What did I get myself into with the Lord?"

We can say, "What did I get myself into with the Lord?" by asking Him to bless us with what we pray to Him for.

We can say, "What did I get myself into with the Lord?" by asking the Lord to give us more faith in Him.

We may not be prepared to receive more faith that can surely put us to the test to pass or not pass with a high grade of the trials that can come our way.

We can say to the Lord, "What did I get myself into for asking You to give me what I may not be strong enough to receive from You?"

The Lord always knows what we can handle, but you and I don't always know if we will be ready to do whatever He tells us to do to uplift and glorify His holy name before brilliant unbelievers.

We can say, "What did I get myself into with the Lord who won't put on us more than what we can bear?"

We can pray to the Lord to bless us to achieve in representing Him and using our spiritual gifts to build up the church.

There is a high cost we must pay for following the Lord on the strait and narrow path that will surely let us know what we get ourselves into with the Lord.

We can very well go beyond our limits in asking the Lord for things that the Lord knows we are not prepared to receive from Him.

The Lord may very well at times answer our prayers and give us what we want and don't need so that we can truly see what we got ourselves into with Him.

We can say and ask ourselves, "What did I get myself into with the Lord who is perfect in all of His ways of doing things in our lives?"

We sinners saved through God's grace can surely regret some things for asking human beings to give us things that can ruin our lives, but the Lord will never ruin our lives by giving us some things that we want and don't need.

We can say, "What did I get myself into with the Lord when He gives us what we ask Him for, even in our ignorance?"

The Lord will never go overboard in giving us anything that will cause our souls to be lost.

The Lord will give us just enough for us to learn a good lesson so we wise up and trust Him to give us what we need so that we don't have to ask ourselves, "What did I get myself into with the Lord?"

The Lord always knows what is best for us.

One Bad Leader

One bad leader in a nation can cause many people to suffer in emotional hardship.

One bad leader in a nation can cause many people to suffer in financial hardship.

One bad leader in a nation can cause many people to suffer in physical hardship.

One bad leader in a nation can cause many people to suffer in economic hardship.

All it takes is one bad leader in a nation to ruin many people's lives.

All it takes is one bad leader in a nation to cause people to have no hope.

All it takes is one bad leader in a nation to cause many people to grieve.

All it takes is one bad leader in a nation to cause many people to get very angry.

All it takes is one bad leader in the church to divide the church.

All it takes is one bad leader in the church to cause some people to leave the church.

All it takes is one bad leader in the church to cause some people to not come to church.

All it takes is one bad leader in the church to form their circle of friends in the church.

We can thank God for giving us His Son, Jesus Christ, who is our one and only true, perfect leader who causes souls to be saved in Him.

Jesus is our Great and Divine Holy Leader who has an eternal nation in heaven where only His righteous people will dwell in.

Our Dreams are Like Watching a Movie

Our dreams are like watching a movie in the unconscious world of our dreams in the night time that we sleep and dream away.

Our dreams are like watching a movie and we don't know what we will see in the next scene of our dream.

Our dreams are like watching a good movie or a bad movie that we can be in to see ourselves having no control over the unconscious world of our dreams that can control us to be in every scene of our dreams.

Our dreams are like watching a movie that can seem like eternity, taking us from one place to another place in our dreams in the night that we sleep and dream away into the morning light.

The movies that film producers make are rehearsed and take a lot of work to produce.

Our dreams are like watching a movie that has no film producers and no rehearsals in the unconscious world of our dreams that we have no clues about what we will dream about in our sleep.

Only the Lord can direct every scene in our dreams to be in His holy will.

Our dreams are like watching a movie but only the Lord knows what we will dream about before we lay down to sleep in the unconscious world of our dreams that also belong to the Lord because no dream is too impossible for the Lord to not understand and give us the true meaning to our dreams.

You and I Will Be

You and I will be criticized for living right unto the Lord Jesus Christ.

You and I will be disliked for living right unto the Lord Jesus Christ.

You and I will be disrespected for living right unto the Lord Jesus Christ.

You and I will be lied on for living right unto the Lord Jesus Christ.

You and I will be put down for living right unto the Lord Jesus Christ.

You and I will be scorned for living right unto the Lord Jesus Christ.

You and I will be talked bad about for living right unto the Lord Jesus Christ.

You and I will be looked down on with contempt for living right unto the Lord Jesus Christ.

You and I will be misunderstood for living right unto the Lord Jesus Christ.

You and I will be falsely accused for living right unto the Lord Jesus Christ.

You and I will be hated for living right unto the Lord Jesus Christ, who was hated by His enemies because Jesus lived right with no sins in His flesh to be the Son of God.

You and I will have enemies for living right unto the Lord Jesus Christ.

You and I will be persecuted for living right unto the Lord Jesus Christ.

You and I will be taken in the wrong way for living right unto the Lord Jesus Christ.

You and I will be despised even by so-called Christians for living right unto the Lord Jesus Christ.

So who can be against You and I who the Lord Jesus Christ is for because of living right unto Him who the devil and his fallen angels and human agents can't ever defeat with all of their evil schemes and deeds?

Love is More

Love is more intelligent than anyone in this world.

Love is more brilliant than anyone in this world.

Love is more genius than anyone in this world.

Love is more convincing than anyone in this world.

Love is more beautiful than any woman in this world.

Love is more strong than any man in this world.

Love is more free than anyone in this world.

Love is more captivating than anything in this world.

Love is more rich than anyone in this world.

Love is more solid than anything in this world.

Love is more rewarding than anything in this world.

Love is more obedient than anyone in this world.

Love is more energetic than anyone in this world.

Love is more serious than anyone in this world.

Love is more healthy than anyone in this world.

Love is more forgiving than anyone in this world.

Love is more friendly than anyone in this world.

Love is more honest than anyone in this world.

Love is more helpful than anyone in this world.

Love is more youthful than anyone in this world.

Love is more smart than anyone in this world.

Love is more genuine than anyone in this world.

Love is more joyful than anyone in this world.

Love is more simple than anyone or anything in this world.

Love is more patient than anyone in this world.

Love is more balanced than anyone in this world.

Love is more good than anyone in this world.

Love is more brave than anyone in this world.

Love is more protective than anyone in this world.

Love is more put together than anyone in this world.

Love is more spiritual than anyone in this world.

Love is more thoughtful than anyone in this world.

Love is more faithful than anyone in this world.

Love is more healing than anyone in this world.

Love is more kind than anyone in this world.

Love is more alive than anyone in this world.

Love is more eye-catching than anyone or anything in this world.

Love is more organized than anyone in this world.

Love is more fast than anyone in this world.

Love is more attentive than anyone in this world.

Love is more careful than anyone in this world.

Love is more wise than anyone in this world.

Love is more active than anyone in this world.

Love is more trustworthy than anyone in this world.

Love is more hopeful than anyone in this world.

Love is more straightforward than anyone in this world.

Love is more interesting than anyone or anything in this world.

Love is more understanding than anyone in this world.

Love is more lasting than anyone or anything in this world.

Love is more humble than anyone in this world.

Love is more peaceful than anyone in this world.

Love is more right than anyone in this world.

Love is more communicating than anyone in this world.

Love comes from God who is love.

Nobody in this world can love anyone more than God, who so loved this world that He gave us His only begotten Son and whosoever believeth in Him shall not perish but have eternal life.

I am a Man

I am a man and I love being a man.

I love talking like a man.

I love dressing like a man.

I am not rich, but I am glad that God created me to be a man.

I love being the man the mirror shows to me every day.

Women are a blessing to me, but I love being a man.

This world would be so lonely without women in it, but I love being a man who loves to see other men talking like men.

I am a man who loves to see other men dressing like men.

I am a man who loves to see other men looking like men.

I am a man who loves to see other men being with a woman like I love being with a woman called my wife, who I love.

I am a man who loves to act like a man every day.

Most of all, I am a Christian man who wants to be like Jesus Christ, who was the only sinless man to be the right example for me to be a man of God.

Most of all, I am a Christian man who loves to treat my neighbors right every day, including every other man and every woman, boy and girl who are my neighbors.

Most of all, I am a Christian man who loves being a Christian man to be like Jesus Christ who was fully man and God who created a man to be a man and a woman to be a woman from the beginning of time here on earth.

Most of all, I am a Christian man who loves to lay up my treasures in heaven because this world is not my home where many men want to be a woman and many women want to be a man.

Most of all, I am a Christian man who loves being like Jesus Christ in this sinful world where I want to help men, women, boys and girls make it to heaven.

Most of all, I am a Christian man who doesn't want to ever be a carnal-minded man again.

I don't miss being that way because being a Christian man is truly being a real man every day.

Most of all, I am a Christian man who has no desire to sin against God willfully because I truly know today that living in sin is of the devil who hates God and every man, woman, boy and girl.

Whether I was being a Christian man or not being a Christian man, it was in God's will for me to be a man because God doesn't make any mistakes in His likeness.

I am glad that God created me to be a man in His likeness that no animal is created in.

Today I am so blessed by God to be a spiritual-minded man that I don't deserve.

I am so glad that Jesus gave up His life on the cross to save me from my sins as if I was the only sinner man in this world.

I am so glad to be a man who Jesus grew up into from a baby boy.

I am so glad to be a Christian man who is no better than any woman — I just have a different role in life.

I am a man who loves to walk like a man in this world where Jesus once walked without sin in His flesh to set the right example for all men to be a man of God and not of the unnatural effects of life.

The same is for every woman to be a woman of God and not of the unnatural effects of life that were not so from the beginning of God creating a man to be a man and a woman to be a woman given in marriage to each other by God, who created a man and woman naturally from the beginning in the Garden of Eden.

I Can Feel Your Presence

I don't see You, O Lord, but when I talk to You I can feel Your presence.

Your presence is strong.

Your presence is peaceful.

Your presence is loving.

Your presence is gentle.

I don't see You, O Lord, but I feel your presence when I pray to You.

Your presence is kind.

Your presence is protective.

Your presence is trustworthy.

Your presence is righteous.

I don't see You, my Lord Jesus Christ, but I feel Your presence in my life.

Your presence is security.

Your presence is loyal.

Your presence is humble.

Your presence is truthful.

Your presence is patience.

Your presence is surety.

Your presence is a blessing to me.

I don't see You, O Lord, but I feel Your presence all around me.

Your presence is life.

Your presence is victory.

Your presence is everything I need.

Your presence is goodness.

Your presence is always on time.

Your presence is beauty.

Your presence is freedom to me.

Your presence is joyful to me.

Your presence is Your Holy Spirit in me.

I don't see You, my Lord and Savior Jesus Christ, but Your presence is eternal life in this temporary world that I am only passing through with Your presence, O Lord, that is so very divine to me every day.

The True Church and the False Church

The true church preaches all the truth and the false church preaches truth mixed with lies.

The true church teaches all the truth and the false church teaches truth mixed with lies.

The true church keeps all the ten Commandments of God and the false church preaches and teaches that we are saved through God's grace and don't have to keep all the ten Commandments of God.

The true church preaches and teaches salvation through Jesus Christ and the false church preaches and teaches salvation through our works.

The true church preaches and teaches Jesus Christ is coming back again on the clouds of glory to raise the righteous dead and change the righteous living from mortal to immortal in the twinkling of an eye.

The false church preaches and teaches that people die and go straight to heaven and they can see you and me and appear before you and me to comfort us.

The true church lives all the truth in the bible, but the false church compromises the truth and does not live all the truth.

The true church preaches and teaches humility unto Jesus Christ, but the false church preaches and teaches prosperity should be the primary goal in a Christian's life.

The true church preaches and teaches God the Father, the Son and the Holy Spirit being the Trinity Godhead, but the false church only preaches and teaches God the Father, leaving out the Son, Jesus Christ, and the Holy Spirit.

The true church preaches and teaches that there is a heaven where Jesus will take us to if we are saved in Him.

The true church also preaches and teaches there is a hell where the devil and his angels and human agents will burn up.

The false church preaches and teaches that there is a purgatory where we will go to if all of our sins are not forgiven by God.

The true church preaches and teaches that sanctification is a lifetime process, but the false church preaches and teaches that once we are saved we are always saved in Jesus.

The true church preaches and teaches that we are made right in God's eyesight through the righteousness of Jesus Christ.

The false church preaches and teaches that we can get ourselves right with God on our own effort.

The true church preaches and teaches that we must believe in Jesus Christ to receive eternal life, but the false church preaches and teaches that we can die and go to heaven and receive eternal life before Jesus comes back again.

Jesus' main reason for coming back again is to give us eternal life in heaven, where we can't go to before Jesus comes back again.

The true church preaches and teaches Jesus Christ, but the false church preaches and teaches the false doctrines of rebellious human beings.

Everybody in the Church

Everybody in the church has their personal struggles, but we should not let them keep us from worshipping the Lord and being rooted and grounded in the Lord.

Everybody in the church has their personal struggles, but we should not let them stop us from respecting one another and loving one another.

Everybody in the church has their personal struggles, but we all can give them to our Lord and Savior Jesus Christ, who overcame every struggle in this world where He once lived without sin in His flesh.

Everybody in the church has their personal struggles, but Jesus can give us the strength to bear them from day to day.

Everybody in the church has their personal struggles, but they are not too hard for Jesus to lighten our burdens and make us strong so we can stand on top of our struggles.

Everybody in the church has their personal struggles, but we should not let them get between us and Jesus.

Everybody in the church has their personal struggles, but we should not let them keep us from giving Jesus our best efforts to love Him and keep His Commandments.

Everybody in the church has their personal struggles that Jesus foreknew before we were born and knew nothing about the things we would go through, especially for His holy name's sake.

Everybody in the church has their personal struggles that Jesus can use for our good to draw us closer and closer to Him, even in some ways that we don't see.

Everybody in the church has their personal struggles that have no power to get us off the pathway to Jesus if we have faith in Jesus to use our personal struggles to encourage us to depend on Him and not on ourselves to overcome our personal struggles that Jesus can truly help us to overcome.

Everybody in the church has their personal struggles, but we can pray to Jesus without ceasing and live for Jesus who our personal struggles can't ever take the place of in our lives if we choose to believe in Jesus Christ over our personal struggles.

Our personal struggles are not more believable than Jesus, who has all power and authority over everybody's personal struggles and public struggles through His blood that was shed on the cross to cleanse us from our sins and save us from our sins.

Everybody in the church and outside the church has their personal struggles and some public struggles, but every true Christian knows what it means to give them all to Jesus who can do all things but fail us.

Everybody in the church has their personal struggles whether they're married or single, young or old, educated or not educated, rich or poor, but Jesus is the head of the church and gives everybody in the church the power to trample over every personal struggle and public struggle to shame the devil who loves to cause everybody in the church to struggle more than anyone who is not in the church.

Everybody in the church has their personal struggles and public struggles, but if we put our hope and trust in Jesus Christ even our struggles will look so peaceful in this troubled world that foolish people put their trust in to give them the victory over their personal struggles and public struggles.

Ignorant

Many people will make ignorant comments about other people who they know nothing about.

Making ignorant comments about people is the same as lying on people.

It's so easy to say wrong things about someone we don't know.

It's so easy to say wrong things about someone who we never talked to.

It's so easy to be ignorant about things that we don't know.

It's so easy to be ignorant about people who we don't know.

Someone who we believe we know can show you and me how ignorant we are for being so wrong about him or her.

It's so easy to be ignorant about ourselves, who don't always know what we will say before we say it.

It's so easy to be ignorant about ourselves, who don't always know what we will do before we do it.

It's so easy to be ignorant about ourselves, who don't always know what we will think before we think it.

It's so easy to be ignorant about ourselves, who don't always know what we will feel before we feel it.

It's so easy to be ignorant about who we don't know and what we don't know from day to day.

Many people back in the bible days were so ignorant about Jesus Christ that they rejected Him out of their ignorance.

Many of those people believed that Jesus was ignorant and couldn't know what was in their hearts.

Many people believe today that Jesus is ignorant and doesn't know their secret sins, but Jesus can surely bring them to light for others to see.

There are Christians who believe that Jesus was ignorant when He didn't know if He could bear being on the cross to save us from our sins.

There are Christians who will assume things about Jesus out of their ignorance and not be in line with God's holy word.

Everybody is ignorant in some kind of way.

The smartest people in this world don't know everything and are ignorant in some kind of way.

There are Christians who will assume that Jesus Christ didn't know all things because He was made flesh to learn about things.

In our fallible minds, ignorance can be a sure thing especially when it comes to the Lord Jesus Christ who we can never learn enough about in our short lifetime here on earth.

There is always something new to learn about the Lord Jesus Christ beyond the writings of the bible scholars who are still ignorant in some kind of way when it comes down to fully knowing how God can work in some mysterious ways.

We all are also ignorant when it comes to the things up in heaven and the things in other worlds that we have never seen.

Nothing will Evolve Beyond God

Things will evolve in this world because of sin that evolves every evil thing.

From the beginning of God's creation in this world, everything was perfect to stay the same way with no existence of any kind of evolvements in this world.

Whatever evolves comes from sin and not from God, who stays the same forever and ever.

Only here on earth things will evolve from the deadly effects of sin that don't exist in heaven and in other worlds where everyone and everything is perfect and will never evolve into the uncertain, temporary changes in life that are only here on earth.

Nothing will evolve beyond God, who gave us His only begotten Son, Jesus Christ, to save us from our sins that instantly evolved in our nature because of Adam disobeying God.

God held Adam so much more accountable for eating that unforbidden fruit.

Nothing will ever evolve beyond God the Father, the Son and the Holy Spirit, who said, "Let us make man and woman in our likeness," before Adam and Eve sinned against God.

After they sinned against God, it affected this whole world and began the process of evolving everything that was created by God.

Many things have evolved in this world because of sin, which caused many things to gradually change and develop into the things that God didn't create from the beginning.

Nothing will ever evolve beyond God, who will one day destroy all sin for nothing to evolve in the new world that God will create to be perfect and nothing will ever evolve there.

Jesus Christ is the Truth to Set Us Free from Living in Sin

Jesus Christ is the truth to set us free from living in sin.

Luck is not the truth to set us free from living in sin.

Magic is not the truth to set us free from living in sin.

Jesus Christ is the truth to set us free from living in sin.

Witchcraft is not the truth to set us free from living in sin.

Horoscopes are not the truth to set us free from living in sin.

Jesus Christ is the truth to set us free from living in sin.

Mediums are not the truth to set us free from living in sin.

Sorcery is not the truth to set us free from living in sin.

Jesus Christ is the truth to set us free from living in sin.

Omens are not the truth to set us free from living in sin.

Spiritualism is not the truth to set us free from living in sin.

Jesus Christ is the truth to set us free from living in sin.

False doctrines are not the truth to set us free from living in sin.

Politics are not the truth to set us free from living in sin.

Jesus Christ is the truth to set us free from living in sin.

Religion is not the truth to set us free from living in sin.

Miracles are not the truth to set us free from living in sin.

Jesus Christ is the truth to set us free from living in sin.

Wealth is not the truth to set us free from living in sin.

Prosperity is not the truth to set us free from living in sin.

Jesus Christ is the truth to set us free from living in sin.

War is not the truth to set us free from living in sin.

Theories are not the truth to set us free from living in sin.

Jesus Christ is the truth to set us free from living in sin.

Philosophies are not the truth to set us free from living in sin.

Phenomena are not the truth to set us free from living in sin.

Jesus Christ is the truth to set us free from living in sin.

Technologies are not the truth to set us free from living in sin.

Science is not the truth to set us free from living in sin.

Jesus Christ is the truth to set us free from living in sin.

Money is not the truth to set us free from living in sin.

Sex is not the truth to set us free from living in sin.

Jesus Christ is the truth to set us free from living in sin.

Human beings are not the truth to set us free from living in sin.

Animals are not the truth to set us free from living in sin.

Jesus Christ is the truth to set us free from living in sin.

Skills are not the truth to set us free from living in sin.

Talents are not the truth to set us free from living in sin.

Jesus Christ is the truth to set us free from living in sin.

Laws are not the truth to set us free from living in sin.

Choices are not the truth to set us free from living in sin.

Jesus Christ is the truth to set us free from living in sin.

Marriage is not the truth to set us free from living in sin.

The church is not the truth to set us free from living in sin.

Jesus Christ is the truth to set us free from living in our sins that Jesus became on the cross He died on to save us from our sins.

Success is not the truth to set us free from living in sin.

Education is not the truth to set us free from living in sin.

Jesus Christ is the living truth to set us free from living in sin that has corrupted everybody to have a sinful nature to sin against God in thoughts, words and in our actions.

Jesus Christ is the living truth to set us free from living in our sins that originated from the devil who hates God and every human being who God created in His likeness

This is the truth that the devil has been trying to make a lie by planting the idea of evolution in the minds of educated and uneducated fools.

Is a Success

Many people will only believe that getting rich is a success.

Many people will only believe that getting a college degree is a success.

Many people will only believe that having a great job is a success.

Many people will only believe that making achievements is a success.

Many people will only believe that winning a championship is a success.

Many people will only believe that winning the lottery is a success.

Many people will only believe that writing a best-seller book is a success.

Many people will only believe that winning an Oscar is a success.

Many people will only believe that winning an Emmy is a success.

Not making the same mistake again is a success.

Keeping your vehicle and your house clean is a success.

Not over-working yourself is a success.

Paying your bills is a success.

Eating right is a success.

Having good hygiene is a success.

Helping someone in need is a success.

Saying the right words is a success.

Dressing decent is a success.

Treating yourself right is a success.

Telling the truth is a success.

Keeping the laws in the land is a success.

Having a good marriage is a success.

Having good friends is a success.

Raising up your children in the right way is a success.

An author getting only one book sold is a success.

Having a good outlook on life is a success.

Saving someone's life is a success.

Doing good things is a success.

If you only win one soul to the Lord Jesus Christ, it is a success for all the angels in heaven to rejoice about.

Loving Jesus and keeping His Commandments is a success.

Being saved in Jesus Christ is a success.

Success can happen in so many ways, but the greatest success is going with Jesus Christ back to heaven when He comes back again on the clouds of glory.

Everyone will not be successful in going with Jesus back to heaven when He comes back again.

No one can ever be more successful than Jesus Christ, who got the victory over death and the grave to give you and me His free gift of eternal life.

No one can ever be more successful than Jesus Christ, who overpowered the devil for never sinning against God when He lived here on earth among sinners and did not ever sin to take this world back from the devil who Adam and Eve gave their dominion over to for sinning against God in the Garden of Eden.

No one can ever be more successful than Jesus Christ, who will successfully write everyone's name in the book of life for being saved in Him.

No one can ever be more successful than Jesus Christ, who will be very successful in showing all the holy saints in heaven why some didn't make it to heaven, especially those who did good works in Jesus' name but had no true conversion to repent and love Jesus and keep His Commandments.

To the Full Extent

No one can keep the law of God to the full extent.

We will break the law of God in a knowing or ignorant way.

The purpose of God's holy law is to show us our sins.

The law of God can't save us from our sins.

Jesus foreknew that the law of God would not save anyone from their sins.

Jesus foreknew that He would have to leave all of heaven to be made flesh without sin and live a sinless life among sinners to show them that He was the only one who could keep the law of God to the full extent.

We sinners were born in sin to break God's holy law even unintentionally on the spur of the moment is something we Christians can do.

Without the law of God, we wouldn't know what sin is and wouldn't know that we disrespected God's character.

God's holy law is the character of God, who can do no evil and no wrong to anyone.

No one in this world can keep the law of God to the full extent, for as long as we live in this sinful world, we will break God's holy law in some kind of way.

We can break God's holy law in our thoughts, words and actions and may not realize it until the Holy Spirit convicts us that we broke God's holy law.

Only Jesus Christ, our Lord and Savior, kept God's holy law to the full extent because He was perfect to have no sins for Him to be truth and grace given to us who don't deserve it.

We are saved through God's grace because of Jesus Christ who gave up His life on the cross to save us from our sins which is something the law of God can't do for us.

Just because the law of God can't save us doesn't meant we have an excuse to not want to try to keep the ten Commandments of God.

We need the Holy Spirit to help us to keep the ten Commandments of God because we cannot keep them on our own strength that will fail us and we will break the law of God in some kind of seen and unseen way.

It's truly God's grace that keeps us from dropping dead as soon as we break God's holy law that points out our sins to us.

Even for people who don't know God's law, God put His law in their hearts so that even a child will feel guilty after telling his or her parents a lie.

Back in the bible days, the Pharisees believed that they were keeping the law of God to the full extent even as they broke them for especially not believing in Jesus Christ, who fulfilled the law of God.

Jesus says, "If you love Me, you will keep My Commandments," but Jesus is not saying that we will never break His Commandments.

We Christians can greatly desire to keep God's Commandments but we will fall short of the glory of God and sin against God even in some ways that we don't see.

Jesus truly knows all who love Him, regardless of having a sinful nature that God's grace hovers over like the sky hovers over all the world.

No one can keep the law of God to the full extent and never break it.

We will have a sinful nature to break God's law.

Our righteousness is like filthy rags because we were born in sin that breaks God's law.

Only the righteousness of Jesus can make us right with God.

The law of God can't make us right with God because the purpose of the law is to show us that sin exists in us to break God's law, which we can do even in an ignorant way no matter how much we know the word of God.

No one has ever kept the full extent of God's law except Jesus Christ, who had no sin in thoughts, words or actions when He lived in this sinful world among sinners like you and me.

Jesus gave us His life on the cross to save us from our sins, and He rose from the grave to give us eternal life that is the full extent of God's love for us.

The purpose of confessing our sins and repenting of our sins is because we have sins to break God's law and not keep the full extent of God's law. ·

We can thank God for His Son, Jesus Christ, who kept the full extent of God's law for you and me to be saved in Him.

We cannot save ourselves because we are cursed by the law of God if there is no grace given to us through Jesus Christ, who is truth and grace from God.

Only Jesus can save us from our sins to the full extent if we love Jesus and want to keep His Commandments — the law of God can't do this.

No matter how much every Christian loves Jesus, you and I will still fall short of the glory of God and have sins to confess and repent of to prove that we break God's holy law.

We true Christians have no desire to want to break God's holy law because we want to love Jesus Christ to the full extent that pleases God, who gives us His Holy Spirit to the full extent.

Jesus says that if we love Him, we will keep His Commandments, but Jesus is not saying that we will never sin against Him ever again.

If we love Him, we must confess our sins unto Him because of breaking God's holy law that is the full extent of God's character.

Our love for Jesus is a lifetime of spiritual growth because there is always more room for us to love Jesus more and more to the full extent.

We can break God's holy law in our thoughts, words, and actions without being aware we're doing it, but that doesn't mean that we don't love Jesus who will wink his eye at our ignorance of what we don't know.

No true Christian will love and obey Jesus to the full extent because we are unaware of sins we don't see that break God's holy law.

Only the righteousness of Jesus Christ will make us right in God's eyesight.

All the right thoughts we think, all the right words we say and all the right deeds we do don't come close to keeping the full extent of God's holy law.

Only the blood of Jesus will cleanse us of our sins that only Jesus can save us from to the full extent.

Jesus is our only living truth and grace to the full extent.

No one's imagination or false theories can override God's holy law, and no one has an excuse to knowingly break Gods' holy law.

No one can keep God's holy law to the full extent, especially if you believe that you can save yourself and enter heaven without believing in Jesus Christ, who can save us from our sins which the law of God can't do.

If we love Jesus, we will want to keep His Commandments.

Only the Holy Spirit can help us to keep God's holy law one day at a time.

We must pray to the full extent and live for Jesus, whose righteousness covers over our best righteousness, which is like filthy rags before God every day.

Because of our sinful nature, we will break God's holy law in some kind of way for the Holy Spirit to convict us to confess and repent of our sins.

I Don't Know What It's Like to have No Sins

I don't know what it's like to have no sins.

Do you know what it's like to have no sins?

I don't know what it's like to never think wrong.

I don't know what it's like to never say something wrong.

I don't know what it's like to never do something wrong.

I don't know what it's like to have no sins.

Do you know what it's like to have no sins?

I don't know what it's like to have never judged anyone.

I don't know what it's like to never have had a bad habit.

I don't know what it's like to have never assumed anything about someone.

I don't know what it's like to have no sins.

Do you know what it's like to have no sins?

I don't know what it's like to never hold a grudge against someone.

I don't know what it's like to never have lusted.

I don't know what it's like to have no sins to confess and repent unto the Lord Jesus Christ.

I don't know what it's like to never make a mistake.

I don't know what it's like to never get angry.

I don't know what it's like to never have been proud.

I don't know what it's like to have no sins.

Do you know what it's like to have no sins?

We were born in sin to have a sinful nature to sin against God in seen and unseen ways.

We can truly thank God for giving us His Son, Jesus Christ, to save us from being lost in our sins if we confess and repent of our sins unto the Lord Jesus Christ.

All who are saved in Jesus will one day know what it's like to have no sins when Jesus comes back again on the clouds of glory.

Jesus will give us all a new immortal body that is completely free from sin, but until then and for as long as we live in this sinful world, we will have sins to confess and repent unto Jesus Christ.

We are all sinners saved through God's grace that we don't deserve, no matter what right things we say and do.

Our righteousness is like filthy rags before a holy and righteous God.

I don't know what it's like to have no sins.

Do you know what it's like to have no sins?

When Jesus lived in this sinful world, He had no sins.

Jesus became sin on the cross to save us from our sins.

Jesus never had a corrupt thought.

Jesus never said one wrong word.

Jesus never did anything wrong when He lived here on earth without sin in His flesh.

He is our Lord and Savior and the Light of the world.

Jesus knows what it's like to have no sins so He can forgive us of our sins.

Jesus knows what it's like to have no sins so he can cleanse us of our sins.

Jesus knows what it's like to have no sins so He can save us from our sins if we confess and repent of our sins unto Him.

I don't know what it's like to have no sins.

Do you know what it's like to have no sins?

I don't' know what it's like to never have doubted God.

What about you?

I don't know what it's like to have never been jealous of anyone.

I don't know what it's like to have never been rude to anyone.

I don't know what it's like to have never hated anyone.

I don't know what it's like to have no sins.

Do you know what it's like to have no sins?

I don't know what it's like to have never eaten too much food.

I don't know what it's like to have never imitated anyone.

I don't know what it's like to have never pretended with anyone.

I don't know what it's like to have no sins.

Do you know what it's like to have no sins?

I don't know what it's like to never talk bad about someone.

I don't know what it's like to never have sinned against God.

Do you know what it's like to have no sins?

I don't know what it's like to never have overworked myself.

I don't know what it's like to never have any bad intentions.

I don't know what it's like to have no sins.

Do you know what it's like to have no sins?

I don't know what it's like to never feel any guilt.

I don't know what it's like to have never been guilty.

I don't know what it's like to have never deceived someone.

I don't know what it's like to have no sins to confess and repent of unto the Lord Jesus Christ.

Do you know what it's like to have no sins to confess and repent unto the Lord Jesus Christ?

I don't know what it's like to never offend someone.

I don't know what it's like to have never broken God's ten Commandments.

I don't know what it's like to never have taken God's grace for an excuse to do my own will.

Do you know what it's like to have no sins that Jesus became on the cross to save us from our sins if we confess our sins and repent and live for Jesus?

I don't know what it's like to never have feared anything or anyone.

I don't know what it's like to never have been wrong.

I don't know what it's like to never have made a bad choice.

I don't know what it's like to have no sins.

Do you know what it's like to have no sins?

I don't know what it's like to have never interrupted someone.

I don't know what it's like to have never wanted to get revenge.

I don't know what it's like to have never brought any hardship on myself.

I don't know what it's like to have never misunderstood someone.

I don't know what it's like to never have done someone wrong.

I don't know what it's like to have no sins.

Do you know what it's like to have no sins?

I don't know what it's like to have never quenched the Holy Spirit.

I don't know what it's like to have never been ignorant.

I don't know what it's like to have never denied Jesus before someone.

I don't know what it's like to have no sins.

Do you know what it's like to have no sins?

I don't know what it's like to have never disobeyed my parents.

I don't know what it's like to have never taken something that didn't belong to me.

I don't know what it's like to have never tried to draw attention to myself.

I don't know what it's like to have no sins.

Do you know what it's like to have no sins?

I don't know what it's like to have never been selfish.

I don't know what it's like to have never fallen short of the glory of God.

I don't know what it's like to have no sins.

Do you know what it's like to have no sins?

I don't know what it's like to have never lived in this world without sin in my flesh.

I don't know what it's like to have never eaten any food that is not good to eat.

I don't know what it's like to have never failed someone.

I don't know what it's like to have never rejected the Lord in some kind of way.

I don't know what it's like to have no sins that I was born in and only Jesus Christ can save me and you from when no one in this world can prove to be without sin to not be a sinner saved through God's grace.

I don't know what it's like to have never grieved.

I don't know what it's like to have never disappointed someone.

I don't know what it's like to have never joked about someone.

I don't know what it's like to have no sins.

Do you know what it's like to have no sins?

I don't know what it's like to have never worried.

I don't know what it's like to have never been sick.

I don't know what it's like to have never felt pain.

I don't know what it's like to have no sins.

Do you know what it's like to have no sins?

I don't know what it's like to have never been anxious.

I don't know what it's like to have never been impatient.

I don't know what it's like to have never forgotten something.

I don't know what it's like to have no sins.

Do you know what it's like to have no sins?

I don't know what it's like to have never changed on someone.

I don't know what it's like to have never pretended.

I don't know what it's like to have never been in trouble.

I don't know what it's like to have never gossiped.

I don't know what it's like to have no sins.

Do you know what it's like to have no sins?

I don't know what it's like to have never been thirsty.

I don't know what it's like to have never been hungry.

I don't know what it's like to have never been in a rush.

I don't know what it's like to have no sins.

Do you know what it's like to have no sins?

I don't know what it's like to have never disliked someone.

I don't know what it's like to have never been careless.

I don't know what it's like to have never wanted what I couldn't have.

I don't know what it's like to have no sins that only Jesus Christ was without when He lived on earth to redeem us back to God.

I don't know what it's like to have never smelled bad.

I don't know what it's like to have no sins.

Do you know what it's like to have no sins, when all sin is bad to God?

I don't know what it's like to have never been unfriendly to someone.

I don't know what it's like to have never lied to God.

I don't know what it's like to have never mistrusted God.

I don't know what it's like to have never sinned against God.

I don't know what it's like to have no sins.

Do You know what it's like to have no sins?

I don't know what it's like to have no sins in this sinful world.

I don't know what it's like to have never said something wrong even on the spur of the moment.

I don't know what it's like to have never done something wrong even on the spur of the moment.

I don't know what it's like to have never questioned God.

I don't know what it's like to have never complained.

I don't know what it's like to have no sins.

Do you know what it's like to have no sins?

I don't know what it's like to have never misinterpreted a bible scripture.

I don't know what it's like to have never given in to the devil's temptations.

I don't know what it's like to have never showed favoritism.

I don't know what it's like to have never lived in darkness.

I don't know what it's like to have never rebelled against God.

I don't know what it's like to have never turned my back on Jesus.

I don't know what it's like to have no sins.

Do you know what it's like to have no sins?

If It's Foolish To

If it's foolish to believe in Jesus Christ, then why should we have even been born?

If it's foolish to put our trust in Jesus Christ, then why should we even be visible to one another?

If it's foolish to worship Jesus Christ, then why should we even live?

If it's foolish to give Jesus the glory and praise, then why should we even prosper in any king of way?

If it's foolish to live for Jesus Christ, then why should we even have a free will?

If it's foolish to have a relationship with Jesus Christ, then why should we even have a heart?

If it's foolish to love Jesus Christ, then why should we even have breath to breathe?

If it's foolish to keep God's Commandments, then why should we even have freedom and justice?

If it's foolish to get to know Jesus Christ, then why should we even open the bible?

If it's foolish to spread the gospel of Jesus Christ, then why should we even have a voice?

If it's foolish to want to be like Jesus Christ, then why should we even believe that there is an afterlife?

If it's foolish to put our hope in Jesus Christ, then why should we even pray?

If it's foolish to be saved in Jesus Christ, then why should we even exist?

If it's foolish to be a Christian, then why should we waste our time going to church that Jesus Christ is the head of to separate the wheat from the tares within the church?

If it's foolish to go through hardships for Jesus' name sake, then why should we even have a conscious to secure our minds to stay on Jesus in our hardships?

What Good is It?

What good is it to be a genius if you don't use it for the Lord?

What good is it to be talented if you don't use it for the Lord?

What good is it to be skillful if you don't use it for the Lord?

What good is it to be wealthy if you don't use it for the Lord?

What good is it to be intelligent if you don't use it for the Lord?

What good is it to be healthy if you don't use it for the Lord?

What good is it to be beautiful if you don't use it for the Lord?

What good is it to be strong if you don't use it for the Lord?

What good is it to be creative if you don't use it for the Lord?

What good is it to be talkative if you don't use it for the Lord?

What good is it to be successful if you don't use it for the Lord?

What good is it to be famous if you don't use it for the Lord?

What good is it to be gifted if you don't use it for the Lord?

What good is it to be prosperous if you don't use it for the Lord?

What good is it to be educated if you don't use it for the Lord?

What good is it to be transparent if you don't use it for the Lord?

What good is it to be great if you don't use it for the Lord?

What good is it to be active if you don't use it for the Lord?

What good is it to be helpful if you don't use it for the Lord?

What good is it to be brave if you don't use it for the Lord?

What good is it to be moral if you don't use it for the Lord?

What good is it to be alive if you and I don't use our lives for the Lord Jesus Christ, who is worthy to be worshipped and praised above all things?

Is Showing People Some Love

Respecting people is showing people some love.

Forgiving people is showing people some love.

Helping people is showing people some love.

Being patient with people is showing people some love.

Being kind to people is showing people some love.

Not judging people is showing people some love.

Being happy for people is showing people some love.

Praying for people is showing people some love.

Being gentle with people is showing people some love.

Showing compassion to people is showing people some love.

Doing the right thing is showing people some love.

Being honest with people is showing people some love.

Listening to people is showing people some love.

Encouraging people is showing people some love.

Motivating people is showing people some love.

Protecting people is showing people some love.

Educating people is showing people some love.

Setting the right example for people is showing people some love.

Giving justice to people is showing people some love.

Accepting people for who they are is showing people some love.

Giving people a smile is showing people some love.

Giving people a handshake is showing people some love.

Being friendly to people is showing people some love.

Making good choices is showing people some love.

Being humble is showing people some love.

Being peaceful is showing people some love.

Minding your own business is showing people some love.

Caring about people is showing people some love.

Feeling sorry for people is showing people some love.

Supporting people is showing people some love.

Being positive with people is showing people some love.

Being transparent with people is showing people some love.

Giving people good advice is showing people some love.

Giving testimonies to people is showing people some love.

Being a witness of Jesus is showing people some love.

Sharing the truth of God's holy word with people is showing people some love.

Spreading the gospel of Jesus Christ is showing people some love.

Treating people right is showing people some love.

Esteeming people is showing people some love.

Holding a door open for people is showing people some love.

Keeping your distance while driving on the road is showing people some love.

Dressing in modest apparel is showing people some love.

Tolerating people is showing people some love.

Being like Jesus is showing people some love.

The Lord Can Truly Look Out for Us

If the Lord can look out for billions of galaxies, then the Lord can truly look out for us.

If the Lord can look out for billions of universes, then the Lord can truly look out for us.

If the Lord can look out for billions of creatures, then the Lord can truly look out for us.

If the Lord can look out for trillions of stars, then the Lord can truly look out for us.

If the Lord can look out for all of the holy angels, then the Lord can truly look out for us.

If the Lord can look out for all of the unfallen worlds, then the Lord can truly look out for us.

The Lord can truly look out for us so much better than we can ever look out for ourselves.

The Lord can truly look out for us in our homes.

The Lord can truly look out for us in our neighborhood.

The Lord can truly look out for us on the road.

The Lord can truly look out for us in the stores.

The Lord can truly look out for us on our job.

The Lord can truly look out for us in the church.

The Lord can truly look out for us wherever we go.

If something bad happens to us, the Lord can truly look out for us to keep that bad situation from being so much worse on us.

The Lord can truly look out for us who don't have the slightest clue about how the Lord is moving an evil thing out of our way.

The Lord can truly look out for us who can forget something that we truly need, but the Lord can truly bring it back to our memory right on time.

The Lord can truly look out for us who can't always look out for ourselves, even in the safest places that the devil can appear in.

The Lord can truly look out for us even in ways that we can't imagine until the Lord opens our eyes to see that it was Him who truly protected us from the evils of the unknown.

The Lord Jesus Christ can truly look out for us who are like a lost sheep in the wilderness for the Lord to call us to hear His voice.

The Lord can truly look out for us who are like a wanderer having no focus on where to go without Jesus leading us to Calvary to redeem us back to God through His death on the cross for our sins.

Jesus rose the third day to truly look out for us to receive eternal life if we repent and turn to Him who is coming back on the clouds of glory.

Back in the Bible Days

Back in the bible days, the scribes and Pharisees called Jesus Christ a blasphemer for saying before them that He is the Son of God.

They believed that Jesus was a false prophet, the devil and a liar for saying to them that He is the Son of God.

The scribes and Pharisees also believed that Jesus was crazy and delusional for saying to them that He is the Son of God.

The scribes and Pharisees called Jesus a blasphemer for saying that He can forgive people of their sins.

Back in the bible days, many people had listened to Jesus speak words with authority like they had never heard before.

Back in the bible days, people were witnesses to the miracles that Jesus performed before their eyes.

Back in the bible days, the Roman soldiers spit on Jesus, beat on Jesus and made fun of Jesus for saying that He is the Son of God.

The scribes and Pharisees had Jesus nailed on the cross for saying that He is the Son of God.

In our time, many people believe that you and I are crazy for believing in Jesus Christ.

In our time, many people believe that you and I are crazy for spreading the gospel of Jesus Christ.

The devil had his human agents back in the bible days and the devil has his human agents today.

The devil and his human agents called Jesus a blasphemer and crucified Jesus back in the bible days.

The devil and his human agents are oppressing you and me with their false accusations against us for being true followers of Jesus Christ today.

The Jesus back in the bible days is the same Jesus who is mocked by unbelievers today.

Those unbelievers will also mock you and me for being true Christians who even pretense Christians will despise in some clever ways.

Voting is Showing that You

Voting is showing that you truly care about who you want to run this nation.

Voting is showing that you are very concerned about other people.

Voting is showing others that you are present in this nation.

Voting is showing that you have a voice.

Voting is showing that you believe addressing your concerns is important.

Voting is showing that you want what is best for your nation.

Voting is showing that you don't live in isolation.

Voting is showing that you are strong in what you believe.

Voting is showing that you have some trust in who you vote for.

Voting is showing that you are bold to express yourself.

Voting is showing that you have hope in your nation.

Voting is showing that you exist in the nation.

Voting is showing your presence in the voting box.

Voting is showing that you care about the welfare of your nation.

Voting is showing that you love your freedom.

It's in God's will for you to vote for loving and honest leaders to govern this nation.

It's in God's will for you to vote for good and trustworthy leaders to govern this nation.

It's God's will for you to vote for God-fearing leaders to govern this nation.

Voting is showing the real you, because who you vote for to represent you in this great nation is who you are, and this nation is great today because God allowed the United States of America to be great.

Voting is showing that you love your nation that only God can truly make better if it's His holy will.

If You Talk Right to People and Treat People Right

If you talk right to people and treat people right, it can cause people to feel good about themselves.

If you talk right to people and treat people right, it can cause you to feel good about yourself.

If you talk right to people and treat people right, it can cause people to think twice about doing something wrong.

If you talk right to people and treat people right, it can cause you to always want to do what is right.

If you talk right to people and treat people right, it can cause people to want to treat themselves right.

If you talk right to people and treat people right, it can cause you to wise up.

If you talk right to people and treat people right, it can cause people to want to talk right and do what is right.

If you talk right to people and treat people right, it can cause you to be a better person.

If you talk right to people and treat people right, it can cause people to feel bad for talking bad to people and treating people bad.

If you talk right to people and treat people right, it can cause you to always want to be good to people.

If you talk right to people and treat people right, it can cause people to want to get the help they need.

If you talk right to people and treat people right, it can cause you to always want to help yourself.

If you talk right to people and treat people right, it can cause people to think right in their minds.

If you talk right to people and treat people right, it can cause you to always want to be positive.

If you talk right to people and treat people right, it can cause people to want to be honest.

If you talk right to people and treat people right, it can cause you to always want to be honest with yourself.

If you talk right to people and treat people right, it can cause people to love and trust you.

If you talk right to people and treat people right, it can cause you to always want to love and trust yourself.

If you talk right to people and treat people right, it can cause people to believe that there is a God.

If you talk right to people and treat people right, it can cause you to believe that there is a God watching over you.

If you talk right to people and treat people right, it can cause people to have some hope to get them through their hardships.

If you talk right to people and treat people right, it can cause you to not give up on hope.

If you talk right to people and treat people right, even some bad people will want to straighten up and live right unto the Lord Jesus Christ.

If you talk right to people and treat people right, it can cause you to want to believe in Jesus Christ, whose righteousness makes you right before God.

If you talk right to people and treat people right, it can cause people to cheer up and not look back on their misfortunes.

If you talk right to people and treat people right, it can cause you to be joyful in being content.

If you talk right to people and treat people right, it can cause people to forgive those who have done them wrong.

If you talk right to people and treat people right, it can cause you to not want to hold grudges.

If you talk right to people and treat people right, it can cause people to feel guilty for talking bad to you and treating you bad.

If you talk right to people and treat people right, it can cause people to feel ashamed for talking bad about you and disrespecting you.

If you talk right to people and treat people right, it can cause people to respect themselves.

If you talk right to people and treat people right, it can cause you to always want to have good motives and intentions.

If you talk right to people and treat people right, it can cause people to want to confess their sins and repent and turn to Jesus Christ.

If you talk right to people and treat people right, it can cause you to want to put Jesus first in your life and give Him all the glory and praise for loving you and helping you to talk right to people and treat people right.

Every word that you and I say right and everything that you and I do right is from the Lord Jesus Christ, not from you and me whose righteousness is like filthy rags before the Lord our God.

If you talk right to people and treat people right, it can cause people to not give you the evil eye look.

If you talk right to people and treat people right, it can cause you to not want to give people the evil eye look.

If you talk right to people and treat people right, it can cause people to be jealous of you for not being like them and showing favoritism to certain people.

If you talk right to people and treat people right, it can cause you to want to be protective like God, who is protective of every soul that belongs to Him.

God loves all souls to be saved in His Son, Jesus Christ, and God doesn't want anyone to be lost in their sins and join the devil and his fallen angels who are on their way to an eternal doom of fire and brimstone.

If you talk right to people and treat people right, it can cause people to want to take good care of themselves.

If you talk right to people and treat people right, it can cause you to want to take good care of yourself.

If you talk right to people and treat people right, it can cause people to want to change for the better.

If you talk right to people and treat people right, it can cause you to want to think good of people.

If you talk right to people and treat people right, it can cause people to want to be like you because you are wise to give God the glory and praise for all the right words that you say and all the right things that you do.

All of the good things we do and say come from the Lord God, not you and me because we are sinners who will sooner or later say something wrong and do something wrong.

God's grace is sufficient in Jesus Christ to save us from our sins and the devil hates for you and me to talk right to people and treat people right.

www.ingramcontent.com/pod-product-compliance
Lightning Source LLC
Chambersburg PA
CBHW071017120626
46546CB00003B/1126